HER BODY, OUR LAWS

ON THE FRONT LINES OF THE ABORTION WAR, FROM EL SALVADOR TO OKLAHOMA

MICHELLE OBERMAN

BEACON PRESS, BOSTON

BEACON PRESS
Boston, Massachusetts
www.beacon.org

Beacon Press books
are published under the auspices of
the Unitarian Universalist Association of Congregations.

21 20 19 18   8 7 6 5 4 3 2 1

This book is printed on acid-free paper that meets the uncoated paper
ANSI/NISO specifications for permanence as revised in 1992.

Some names and other identifying characteristics of people mentioned
in this work have been changed to protect their identities.

Text design and composition by Kim Arney

Library of Congress Cataloging-in-Publication Data

Names: Oberman, Michelle, author.
Title: Her body, our laws : on the front lines of the abortion war, from El
    Salvador to Oklahoma / Michelle Oberman.
Description: Boston : Beacon Press, 2018. | Includes bibliographical
    references and index.
Identifiers: LCCN 2017041184 (print) | LCCN 2017043325 (ebook) |
    ISBN 9780807045534 (ebook) | ISBN 9780807045527 (hardback)
Subjects: LCSH: Abortion—Case studies. | Abortion—Law and legislation—
    Case studies. | Women drug addicts—Case studies. | Reproductive
    rights—Case studies. | BISAC: SOCIAL SCIENCE / Abortion & Birth
    Control. | LAW / Gender & the Law. | HEALTH & FITNESS /
    Pregnancy & Childbirth.
Classification: LCC RG734 (ebook) | LCC RG734 .O34 2018 (print) |
    DDC 362.1988/8—dc23
LC record available at https://lccn.loc.gov/2017041184

*To Hermana Peggy O'Neill of Suchitoto,
El Salvador, and to the women of Birth Choice, Oklahoma City,
Oklahoma, and Access Women's Health Justice, Oakland,
California. Across many divides, you are kindred spirits, seeing
with the heart, laboring always toward the good.*

———————

*And to the memory of Beatriz Garcia,
who died October 8, 2017, at age twenty-six, from
complications of lupus and from the particular cruelty with
which the forces of poverty, class, education, power,
and gender collided to shape her destiny.*

As a woman, I have no country. . . . As a woman my country is the whole world.

—VIRGINIA WOOLF, *Three Guineas*

CONTENTS

Author's Note   ix

Introduction   1

1   Beatriz and Her Case   13

2   Assessing the Impact of El Salvador's Abortion Ban   43

3   The Reddest State: Oklahoma's Long Battle Over Abortion Law   69

4   The Abortion-Minded Woman and the Law   97

5   America After *Roe*   119

    Conclusion: Parting Thoughts on Leaving Behind
    the Abortion War   139

Acknowledgments   143

Notes   145

Index   167

AUTHOR'S NOTE

I interviewed scores of people over the course of this project, taping some conversations and taking copious notes in all cases. For the sake of readability, I've related some of these encounters as dialogues, complete with quotation marks. Although the ideas and words I use are faithful to the speaker's comments, as recorded in my notes, the dialogues themselves are not direct quotes nor should they be read as such. (Original interview notes from Marina, and from all others mentioned in this book, are on file with the author.)

In this book, I refer to people by the terms they use to describe themselves. I do so out of courtesy for their integrity, and also because I do not think it is constructive to wage a battle over abortion by name-calling. For this reason, I use the terms "pro-life" and "pro-choice," rather than the terms each side often uses when referencing the other.

INTRODUCTION

I am a collector of stories about women's dark secrets. In my work as a law professor, I've studied pregnant women who abuse drugs. I've written articles about postpartum depression and the law, and authored two books about mothers who have killed their children.

I'm compelled by the despair at the heart of these stories, propelled by a belief that if we understand why things go wrong, we will find ways to stop them from happening.

To be sure, there's also a prurient aspect to my fascination. These stories are deeply entwined with sex, after all, and stories about sex are almost always interesting.

In retrospect, it's clear that my fascination with these sad stories began years ago, in my freshman year of college, when I started volunteering at Planned Parenthood. I'd gone there by myself to get fitted for a diaphragm. It felt like the first truly adult thing I'd done in my life: getting contraception. The women there were kind, and they reinforced my sense of having crossed over into not only adulthood but also womanhood.

Every Saturday morning, I crossed the picket lines for my four-hour shift with the women in the abortion clinic's recovery room. There were six recliners in a semicircle around the table where I sat, arranging crackers, juice, and pamphlets describing various forms of family planning. My job was to make sure no one left without contraception. We half-joked about never wanting to see them again.

Women choose abortion for a multitude of reasons, and yet, a sense of desperation is almost always present among them. The decision to end a pregnancy arises in response to the circumstances of one's life. The stories the women told me, as they rested before resuming their lives, were as varied as they were poignant.

I listened to their descriptions of the forces that shaped their decisions, making the abortion seem right, or even inevitable. I could see the way those same forces shaped my own life. Money, love, safety, shelter, health. . . . One experiences each of these things in an intensely personal, direct way: one has more or less, enough or nowhere near enough of them to thrive. But the way these forces come together in the crisis of an unplanned pregnancy lets you see them in stark relief.

The women's stories made visible the things that were going right in my life—the things I relied upon in order to make my way. Their tales were cautionary ones: their lives often seemed ordinary, too. Their stories could easily have been my own. Through their stories, then, I came to understand the way women experience vulnerability around sex.

Perhaps I intended to make a political statement by choosing to volunteer at Planned Parenthood. Yet, what I remember most about the work, which I did off and on in my twenties and thirties, has little to do with an explicit feminist agenda. It wasn't my politics that kept me going back to the clinic, week after week. I kept coming back because the women's stories populated my imagination, shaping my understanding of how it is to be a woman. I mean that their stories showed me the "most obvious, important realities," which, as David Foster Wallace notes in his parable about fish in water, are often the ones that are hardest to see.

There are two young fish swimming along and they happen to meet an older fish swimming the other way, who nods at them and says, "Morning, boys. How's the water?" And the two young fish swim on for a bit, and then eventually one of them looks over at the other and goes, "What the hell is water?"[1]

After I finished law school, I went to work at Loyola, a Catholic university in Chicago. It was there that I first came to know, at more than a superficial level, people who spoke openly of their deep moral opposition to abortion. I began teaching medical ethics, thriving on the difficult conversations, fascinated by the variety of opinions sparked by the stories around which I structured discussion.

It was the 1990s, and the media were consumed with pregnant women who used illegal drugs. Fear of a generation of crack babies animated the public imagination. The news stories evoked images of mostly black women who were portrayed as slutty and irresponsible, busy chasing their high rather than getting clean, if only for the sake of their unborn child. The solution, to some, was to prosecute them for child abuse.

The stories I knew from the abortion clinic were filled with the messy reasons why women have sex without contraception, even though they do not want to get pregnant. My hunch was that the truth about pregnant addicts was more complicated. I began collecting stories from drug rehabilitation centers, from doctors, from child abuse experts, and from the women themselves.[2]

It turned out that sex and drugs went hand in hand. Female addicts get pregnant because sex plays a central role in how they get the drugs they need. They have sex for money, they have sex in exchange for drugs, they have sex with their dealers. For many addicted women, sex has been part of the way they navigate their risky world since they were children. Female addicts are survivors of immense violence and trauma. Studies estimate that somewhere around 70 percent of them have been victims of childhood sexual abuse.[3]

Most drug-addicted women don't use drugs because they like to party, but rather because they want to be numb. Their responses to pregnancy are complicated. Unlike the callous depiction in the media, these women often want to be mothers. Actually, they want to be good mothers. Many see in a baby the prospect of unconditional love, of a new beginning, of a positive identity for themselves as mothers. Many already have lost children to the foster care system. They know the risks of losing yet another child if they continue using drugs, yet still they hold out hope that their unborn child might provide the change they so desperately want.

True, some of these women lack access to abortion, either because any money they have goes to feed their addiction or because they don't recognize their pregnancy until it's too far advanced for an abortion. But the bigger problem underlying the 1990s crisis of perinatal addiction was not that these addicts didn't have access to abortion, but rather that they didn't have access to drug rehabilitation programs. Their cases were too complex for programs developed for single men, too fraught with risk of harm to the fetus and potential liability. The overwhelming majority of drug treatment programs didn't accept pregnant women.

Once I understood their stories, it seemed obvious to me that prosecuting them wouldn't solve the problem. What we needed was an approach built upon our knowledge of addiction, one that paved a path to recovery.

It was 1992. The abortion war was raging in the United States. There were battles over parental notification laws, over clinic protesters, over the timing of viability. The US Supreme Court replaced *Roe v. Wade*'s trimester approach with the *Planned Parenthood v. Casey* decision, which created the "undue burden test." So long as they didn't create too much hardship for women seeking to exercise their constitutional right to terminate an unwanted pregnancy, states could use their power to encourage women to carry to term.

The battle intensified. Both sides argued with righteous indignation, appalled at the immorality or hypocrisy of their opponents.

As a law professor, I followed the legal debates closely, reading every decision. The struggle over abortion—the war—is deadly serious. Yet, the noisy debate over abortion law didn't seem all that connected to my research. That is to say, abortion's legal status didn't make much of a difference in the lives of pregnant addicts.

Abortion law was even less relevant to the new set of stories I'd started collecting: those of women who killed their children. It seems only logical to infer that a mother who kills her child must have been someone who wanted an abortion but, for some reason, couldn't get one. But it turns out that's totally wrong. These cases are complicated in ways that have almost nothing to do with abortion.

I began noticing news reports of mothers who kill following a call I received from a small-town defense lawyer seeking medical-legal experts to help defend a teenager accused of killing her baby by delivering it into a toilet. The girl claimed she didn't know she was pregnant. Over the next several years, I noticed so many similar stories that I began collecting them.

The Internet, even in its infancy, made it possible to track news items from around the country. I began searching for articles. I wanted to understand how a girl might conceal her pregnancy and what would make her deliver her baby at home, in the toilet. I felt that understanding why these cases happened would help me formulate my ideas about how the legal system ought to respond. I found hundreds of news stories. I met with doctors, spoke to experts, and ultimately interviewed women in prison for this crime.

I've spent decades studying these stories. They are messy and varied, but one thing is certain: these cases don't involve women who wanted to terminate their pregnancies but lacked access to legalized abortion. Instead, they involve stories like that of a sixteen-year-old whose case came my way. Eva was living with her uncle and his fiancée after her mother told her there wasn't room in her apartment.[4] Starving for love, yet certain she'd have nowhere to live if she had a baby, she spent the months waiting for someone to notice she was pregnant. No one said anything—not her father or stepmother, who later said they'd suspected she was pregnant, nor her mother, nor her friends, to whom she'd confided her predicament. In the end, she had her baby alone, on a toilet. The baby drowned.

When we spoke, I asked Eva why she didn't have an abortion. It was legal, and she could have consented without her parents' permission. It wasn't that she lacked the money, she said. Her ex-boyfriend had even offered to pay for it, before he stopped talking to her. But she didn't want an abortion. She didn't want to kill her best chance at feeling connected and loved.

The same desire to be a mother—to be a good mother—surfaced when I was researching mothers imprisoned for killing their children. Working with Dr. Cheryl Meyer, a psychologist and lawyer, I interviewed forty women in an Ohio prison for having killed their children. These women were incarcerated for crimes like beating their children and then failing to take them to the hospital in time, or standing by while their boyfriend beat their child to death.

Yet they bristled when asked whether they'd considered having an abortion. They wanted to be mothers. Most of their babies were simply victims of the chaos in their mothers' lives. The mothers didn't wish them dead. Most began our conversations about the child they'd been convicted of killing by saying, "Being a mother is the single most important thing in my life."

I was coming to believe that, for the most vulnerable and marginalized women, abortion's legal status hardly mattered. There are women who live with a chaos so profound that despair predates the unplanned pregnancy. Women for whom the notion of a planned pregnancy is itself almost meaningless.

The abortion battle has always raged in the background of my research. In the early twenty-first century, it grew louder, as lawmakers showed their opposition to abortion by enacting a broad swath of abortion-related laws.[5] As a law professor, it seemed to me that I should have been more engaged by the battle over abortion laws. But the sad stories I'd spent a lifetime gathering made me a skeptic about the hyperbolic promises of "choice" and "life."

I thought of a woman I met in prison for killing her two-year-old child. She'd begun raising her four younger siblings at age nine, because her parents were addicts. My hunch is that by the time she became pregnant, at fourteen, no amount of access to safe, affordable abortion would have tugged her to safety.[6]

The abortion debate doesn't concern itself with stories like hers; it ignores the lives of pregnant addicts. Yet, the lives of these women are circumscribed by norms and laws governing sex and motherhood. How much, I wondered, did it matter if abortion was illegal?

In 2008, I went to Chile to try answering this question. At the time, Chile had the world's strictest law against abortion—making it a crime in all cases, without exception. I wanted to learn whether banning abortion shaped the circumstances or frequency of cases involving mothers who kill.

I had clear expectations about what I would find in a country that outlawed abortion. I imagined that, in addition to tragic stories surrounding US mothers who kill, I would find cases of women who were driven to their crimes because they couldn't get a legal abortion.

I knew the studies of what happened in the United States, before legalized abortion. There would be hospital wards overflowing with women who had septic shock or had perforated their uteruses by trying to induce abortions with hangers.

Once I got to Chile, though, I became distracted. Nothing looked as I'd expected. There were no hospitals filled with women injured from illegal abortions, no epidemic of cases involving women who abandoned their newborns to die.

I shifted from worrying about mothers who kill their children to trying to understand what was going on with abortion in Chile. I found law professor Lidia Casas, a prominent Chilean lawyer who has devoted her career to challenging Chile's abortion ban. She explained that the ban was one of the final acts of the brutal dictator Augusto Pinochet when leaving office in 1988.

"Perhaps he wanted to leave a legacy other than having ordered the killing of tens of thousands of his political opponents," she suggested with a grim smile.

His legacy seemed to be intact. Other than Casas, no one seemed terribly interested in changing the law. Every day on my way to the subway, I passed the Castrense Cathedral, adorned with a plaque from 1994 that read "To the Memory of Children Assassinated Before Birth."

With Casas's help, I began making sense of how the abortion ban worked in practice. I met Dr. Ramiro Molina, director of the country's only adolescent health clinic, located within a public hospital that serves Santiago's poorest residents. When I asked him to tell me about unplanned pregnancy and abortions in Chile, he said, "Abortion is a non-issue in Chile. You can buy abortion drugs on the street anytime you like."

The abortion drug most widely available in Chile is misoprostol. It's only part of the formulation of the more effective abortion drug used in the United States. Even so, taken alone and within the first twelve weeks of a pregnancy, misoprostol will bring on a miscarriage in 90 percent of cases. Unless the bleeding is severe, there's no need to see a doctor.

I asked him where women found the drug. He opened his computer and plugged "misoprostol" into a search engine. Thousands of vendors appeared at the click of a mouse.

In spite of its being completely against the law, abortion in Chile is commonplace. Because it is illegal, estimates of how many abortions take place every year in Chile vary widely. But all agree that tens of thousands of women have abortions there every year.[7]

In contrast to the stories from US history, or from places where medical abortion is largely unavailable, in Chile the high rates of illegal abortions don't appear to have led to high rates of maternal mortality.[8] In fact, experts agree that fewer women die from illegal abortions now than they did fifty years ago, before the ban.[9]

If abortion remained commonplace in spite of being illegal, I wondered how the abortion law was enforced. Who gets prosecuted for the crime of illegal abortion when tens of thousands of women have them every year?

As both a defense lawyer and a law professor, Casas knew the answer. She'd studied prosecution patterns since the ban took effect and found evidence suggesting that prosecution rates declined, rather than increased, in the years since the abortion ban took effect.[10] Furthermore, when the state prosecuted women or doctors for illegal abortion,

Casas's research showed that conviction rates were low and punishment was light.

What was the purpose of the law, I wondered, if it wasn't going to be enforced? As an answer, she introduced me to her former client, Marina.

Casas had defended Marina in the summer of 2007, when Marina was prosecuted for the crime of abortion. Marina was one of only a handful of women prosecuted for abortion in Chile that year. She was caught when a sensational news channel ran a sting operation, filming women as they entered an abortion doctor's office, and as they exited. Afterward, the reporters approached each of the women individually, showed them the film, and offered them a deal: confess to us on film and we will tell the district attorney to make a plea agreement with you. Most of them confessed, but they all were prosecuted anyway.

"My story was the most interesting to the press because I was the oldest," Marina told me. "I was almost forty, and I had a teenage daughter. I'd been living overseas for twenty years, and had only recently returned to Chile."

"When I became pregnant, I was so ashamed," Marina continued. "My daughter could have such a thing happen to her, but not a grown woman like me. My period had been irregular for the past few years. I didn't even notice it wasn't coming."

"I made phone calls to old girlfriends," Marina continued. "I had been gone so long. I knew I couldn't keep it, though, so I called until a friend of a friend gave me a name."

"How much did it cost you?"

"$5,000. The rich women fly to Miami, you know. Women like me stay here. It costs between $5,000 and $8,000. Really, it's cheaper to fly to Miami. But then it's so obvious. And besides, there was my work and my daughter, so I never really considered it."

Marina was convicted. She had been caught on film. Yet, even though the crime carries a sentence of up to five years, like other women convicted of abortion in recent years in Chile, Marina did not have to go to prison. She didn't even have to be on probation, nor was she required to comply with any particular court orders. Marina's sentence was suspended. After the trial, Marina went free.

I returned to the United States baffled by the Chilean abortion law. If abortion was tantamount to murder under the law, how could the country be at peace with the high rates of illegal abortion and the low rates of law enforcement?

The following year, in 2009, I attended the first binational meeting of El Salvadoran and Nicaraguan abortion-rights' activists. Like Chile, both of these countries ban abortion without exception. The bans were relatively new; when El Salvador banned abortion in 1998, it became the world's third country, along with Chile and Malta, to do so. Nicaragua joined that number in 2004. In both countries, as in Chile, the bans intensified already restrictive abortion laws, which for decades had outlawed abortion except in cases of threat to maternal life or health, rape or incest, or fetal anomaly.

Lawyers, doctors, and activists from the two countries met to share information about the law's impact—largely on the poorest women in both countries—and to discuss strategies for law reform. At the gathering, it became clear that the situation in El Salvador was different from that in Nicaragua and Chile. In El Salvador, the government actively attempted to enforce the law. I heard stories of women who were shackled to hospital beds, still hemorrhaging, after seeking care in emergency rooms. In the ten years since the ban took effect, scores of women had been imprisoned for crimes related to illegal abortion.

I wanted to know more. I returned to the United States and secured funding for a new research project, looking at the impact of criminalizing abortion in the twenty-first century. Over the next five years, I returned nine times to El Salvador.

At some point during the weeks and months I spent in El Salvador, I realized I was not simply researching the impact of El Salvador's abortion ban. Instead, I was trying to solve the same puzzle in El Salvador that I'd encountered in Chile: there was widespread political support for the ban, yet illegal abortion was commonplace and prosecutions were so sporadic that it was hard to imagine they deterred women from terminating their pregnancies.

Over the six years during which I researched and wrote this book—2010–2016—the battle over abortion law in El Salvador intensified. Advocates for and against El Salvador's abortion ban garnered attention within the country and around the world as they fought over the law. The more pitched the battle, the more familiar it felt to me, until finally I realized that the war over abortion, whether in El Salvador or in the United States, takes on the same form: it becomes a struggle over abortion law.

Watching the abortion war play out in El Salvador, I slowly realized that, for all the fighting over abortion laws, once you get past the slogans, neither side seems to spend much time considering what they're fighting for.

I found I was writing a book about how and why and how much and to whom abortion laws matter. And to answer those questions, it would help to have a deeper understanding of the values and hopes that animated the people in the country I knew best.

Even as I was finishing my research in El Salvador, I set about investigating abortion politics in the United States. I started by visiting Oklahoma, one of the most pro-life US states. There, I came to know lawyers and advocates who have devoted much of their lives to fighting to make abortion once again a crime. Closer to home, I met with Californian abortion-rights scholars and activists. From them, I learned not only what they think is at stake in the fight over abortion laws, but also what issues the abortion war has left behind.

It was here in the United States, in the overwhelmingly pro-choice state of California, that I became convinced of the truth in my hunch, formed years ago when studying pregnant addicts and mothers who killed their children. For the most vulnerable girls and women, abortion's legal status doesn't make all that much difference.

This book is the result of my long journey through the abortion war. I hesitate to call it one war, rather than many. After all, my journey has taken me to different countries, where I've met people with vastly different life experiences and wide-ranging conceptions about abortion's morality. I've studied the laws of jurisdictions all over the world.

Yet, I've come away certain of at least one thing: the battle lines over abortion are being drawn with laws. There is one war over abortion, and laws are the weapons with which it is fought.

This book calls our collective attention to the fundamental, yet unasked question underlying our abortion war: what is it about abortion that we think will be changed by way of abortion laws?

This question is unasked because our discourse about abortion is largely limited to announcing one's position on abortion's legality. All that the abortion war requires of us is that we pick our side on the question of legality. As if the question of how and why abortion laws matter was beside the point.

I consider myself pro-choice. That is to say, I support a woman's unfettered right to choose to terminate a pregnancy. But this book is not written to persuade you to keep or change your opinion about whether abortion should be legal. Rather, it's to invite you to consider the ways in which abortion law matters—to encourage you to reconsider the utility of the terms of our debate, if not the debate itself.

I am issuing not so much an invitation, in the spirit of intellectual inquiry, but more of an exhortation, offered in the names of the countless women whose stories I carry with me. Because year after year, the war over abortion law consumes vast resources, not only in the United States but in countries worldwide. And year after year, that war does little to alter the concrete factors that shape whether a woman will consider having an abortion.

ONE

BEATRIZ AND HER CASE

I want to start our search into how abortion law matters by taking you to El Salvador. It has the strictest laws against abortion in the world: abortion is never legal there, not even if a woman needs one to save her life.

In spring 2013, a case arose that put the abortion ban to the test. A woman known only as Beatriz was just over three months pregnant when doctors learned that her fetus didn't have a brain. It had a rare condition called "anencephaly," which is always fatal. Humans cannot live without a brain; if her baby did not die in utero, it would die shortly after birth. To make matters worse, Beatriz's health status was extremely fragile because she had lupus—an incurable disease that causes the body's immune system to attack its own organs. Two years earlier, she had almost died and her kidneys became permanently impaired as a result of her pregnancy with her first child. Her doctors warned that she could easily die if she became pregnant again.

With no hope for her fetus's survival and her life in danger, anywhere else in the world, Beatriz would have been advised to have an abortion. Yet because the law in El Salvador completely prohibits abortion, that option was foreclosed.

Beatriz petitioned the Salvadoran government for permission to terminate her pregnancy. Her case triggered an international firestorm. Within El Salvador, branches of government took aim at one another. Around the world, advocates on both sides of the abortion war circulated news stories, petitions, and videos, pleading for support.

I followed Beatriz's case from the United States as it made its way through the Salvadoran legal system, stretching on for weeks and then months. Beatriz was seven-months pregnant by the time the Salvadoran Supreme Court denied her petition, concluding that an abortion was unnecessary because her life was not at imminent risk. Then, two weeks later, her doctors performed an emergency cesarean section. Beatriz's daughter died shortly after birth.

Neither side was surprised by the baby's death. The fact that the fetus was doomed was understood from the start. It was one of the only facts on which both sides agreed.

At the most basic level, the outcome in Beatriz's case seems perverse. For the sake of a fetus that would never live, Salvadoran law forced Beatriz to endure months of physical and psychological pain, gravely risking her own health and life.

But Beatriz's case cannot be understood simply at this basic level. As we will see in this chapter, Beatriz's case played out not only in the legal sphere, but also in the court of public opinion. For those who opposed the abortion law, her case was the utmost example of the law's absurdity, and a perfect case with which to challenge the ban. For those who supported the ban, Beatriz's case tested the moral and legal integrity of their position that life begins at conception. Allowing Beatriz an abortion would have made that belief seem negotiable.

I went to El Salvador to try to understand Beatriz's case, with its puzzling outcome. I came home with many stories that help to explain why things unfolded as they did. Read together, these stories permit us to understand, through fresh eyes, the purpose and the significance of abortion laws. Just as importantly, they shed light on the limited extent to which the law makes a difference in the lives of women like Beatriz.

BEATRIZ'S PREDICAMENT

Dr. Guillermo Ortiz first met Beatriz in 2011, when she was pregnant with her son, Claudio, who was two years old when the story with which we are concerned began. Ortiz is one of El Salvador's leading perinatologists, specializing in managing high-risk pregnancies, and working at La Maternidad, the country's main public hospital for obstetrics and gynecology.

"That first pregnancy was terrible," he told me. "She almost died. She got to seven-and-a-half months, but then her lungs filled with fluid and we couldn't control her blood pressure."[1]

Beatriz had been hospitalized for several months, beginning at twenty weeks of pregnancy. Her doctors worked around the clock to keep her stable so that her fetus could develop long enough that it would be able to survive outside of the womb. Beatriz was on six different medications to control her blood pressure, but finally she developed preeclampsia—a condition in which blood pressure becomes life-threateningly high, damaging other organs. Beatriz's kidneys were failing.

"We gave her an emergency cesarean section," Dr. Ortiz told me. "The newborn spent more than a month in the ICU, but he was in good condition. And we saved Beatriz's life. But as a result of that pregnancy, she now has chronic hypertension and a kidney dysfunction called lupus nephritis."

Her second pregnancy was more complicated from the start. In February 2013, suspecting she might be pregnant, Beatriz stopped taking her lupus medicine, which put her into a medical crisis. Her skin was covered with painful eruptions; she had hypertension, and her damaged kidneys were spilling protein into her urine, leaving her blood and body severely weakened.

By the time her lupus doctors verified her pregnancy and referred her to La Maternidad, she was eleven weeks pregnant and very ill.

So Beatriz found herself back at La Maternidad, pregnant and panicked because she knew too well how close she'd come to dying during her first pregnancy.

"We reassured her that we would do everything we could to keep her safe and healthy," Ortiz told me. "The surprise came a few weeks later, when we did the ultrasound and realized the fetus was anencephalic. So the probability of its survival, here and in any other hospital in the world, is zero. I tell you this because there are those who are confused by the terminology. Anencephaly is related to conditions such as microcephaly or hydrocephaly. And with those conditions, there is a possibility of survival. So there were those who said, 'I know of a case in which the baby survived.' But that's not anencephaly."

"What were your options, once you realized the fetus didn't have a brain and couldn't survive?" I asked.

"When we realized it had no chance of survival, and that the only thing we'd accomplish by continuing the pregnancy is to risk Beatriz's life, we talked to her."

The doctors told Beatriz and her mother about the risks she would face if she carried this pregnancy to term. There were all the life-threatening complications she knew firsthand from her first pregnancy: kidney failure, preeclampsia, stroke, blood clots, and more. In addition, there were risks due to the fact that the fetus was anencephalic. She would have to be hospitalized until she had the baby.

Otiz said, "She was around fourteen weeks pregnant at that point. Her situation was even more serious because her first delivery had required a cesarean section. We knew it was less risky to interrupt an early pregnancy; it was much safer than waiting to do another cesarean section, with its own risks, in addition to the risks from the lupus. We convened a meeting of the medical committee, which is what we do when there is a challenging case. We call together all the relevant experts: intensive care, obstetricians, and neonatologists, to discuss options and set a plan. In this case, we all agreed that interruption was the ideal plan."

Beatriz agreed and asked the doctors to perform the "interruption," as abortion is called there.

Ortiz continued, "But when we talked with the hospital attorney, he told us that our proposed 'interruption' put us at risk of violating the law. We sent him to consult with legal experts, including the Fiscalia de la Republica [the governmental office overseeing all prosecutions], a human rights lawyer, a family law judge, but none supported an interpretation of the law that permitted us to interrupt pregnancy. None of them said, 'Do it. We'll support you.'"

BEATRIZ'S DOCTORS' PREDICAMENT

Beatriz's request that her doctors terminate her pregnancy posed a legal dilemma. In 1998, El Salvador changed its penal code from a law permitting legal abortions in cases of rape, incest, or threat to maternal health or life to a law banning abortions in all cases.[2] There is no way to legally end a pregnancy in El Salvador, even one like Beatriz's, in which the fetus will not survive outside the womb.

At the same time, El Salvador's constitution guarantees a pregnant woman the same right to life promised to all citizens, such that the doctors who fail to provide a dying patient with life-saving treatment violate the patient's fundamental rights. Because Beatriz's doctors believed her illness threatened her life, Beatriz's case forced the state to grapple with two competing rights to life. Under Salvadoran law, both Beatriz and the fetus she carried had a right to life.

It turns out that doctors have been navigating this ambiguity at a practical level since 1998, when abortion was banned. One of the most vivid examples of the impact of the ban on abortion is seen in the way it shapes how doctors treat high-risk pregnancies.

Ortiz described the approach he and his colleagues use when treating very ill pregnant women. He calls it "conservative treatment":

> When we look to international health literature to guide us about how best to treat certain illnesses—for example, metastatic breast cancer and an early pregnancy—the experts suggest terminating pregnancy. We can't follow that suggestion, though. And, when we seek guidance on how to proceed without terminating the pregnancy, there's none to be had. And so we forge our own experience. . . . For example, in

the case of cancer, we give the lowest doses of chemo, rather than give her the best, most effective treatment, because we have to worry about the fetus.[3]

Ortiz's discomfort with conservative treatment is that it isn't really treatment at all. In the absence of established medical guidelines, let alone systematic research into how or whether breast cancer chemo-therapy works when given at low doses to pregnant women, El Salvador is conducting an ongoing, unregulated medical experiment on this segment of its population—women and fetuses alike.

The impact of conservative treatment is perhaps most readily observed in the way Salvadoran doctors treat ectopic pregnancy. An ectopic pregnancy occurs when a fertilized egg gets stuck in the fallopian tube, rather than moving down into the woman's uterus. Instead of being able to grow, as it would in the uterus, the egg starts to develop inside of the tube, which is small and incapable of supporting a pregnancy. There is no chance it will develop into a fetus, let alone become a live baby. Left to grow, within twelve to sixteen weeks, the embryo explodes, destroying the tube, leading the woman to bleed profusely, and triggering health complications ranging from the risk of stroke to kidney damage and even death.[4] In addition, losing a fallopian tube may limit her ability to conceive in the future. Ectopic pregnancies are not rare. Between 2005 and 2009, the most recent years for which statistics are available, the Salvadoran Ministry of Health estimates that there were 1,567 ectopic pregnancies and another 46 abdominal pregnancies.[5]

Another of Beatriz's doctors described, with evident frustration, the way he treats ectopic pregnancies. You hospitalize the woman and then

you watch her night and day with scans, and the minute it bursts, you operate and take the tube. . . . She's in imminent risk of dying and I've got the responsibility of saving her life. Waiting is totally contrary to medical principles. It's no different from having an aneurism in the brain; one can see from scans that it's growing and growing. Why would you wait until it explodes? There's no single medical principle that would justify waiting.[6]

I pushed the doctor to clarify the connection between the ban on abortion and this approach to treating ectopic pregnancies—embryos that would never survive. His reason reflected the central puzzle of Beatriz's case: if it's a person from the moment of conception, then deliberately killing the embryo, let alone the fetus, could be considered homicide.

If the hospital lawyers interpret the law to require waiting for a tube to explode, rather than removing an ectopic pregnancy, it's easy to see why they similarly would have advised the doctors against terminating Beatriz's pregnancy. She was already fourteen weeks along; she was carrying a fetus, not merely an embryo. And in spite of its inevitable demise, her fetus was growing larger every day.

EL SALVADOR'S RESPONSE TO BEATRIZ'S REQUEST FOR AN ABORTION

When it became clear that the doctors would not terminate her pregnancy, one of her nurses reached out to a local women's group that found Beatriz a lawyer. In April, when Beatriz was seventeen weeks pregnant, the lawyer filed a petition asking the court for permission to terminate her pregnancy. The government took fifty-five days to reach a decision in her case, by which point she was nearly seven-months pregnant.

By examining the legal proceedings in the context of the climate in which they played out, it is easy to see the extent to which Beatriz's predicament came to stand for far more than the simple legal question of whether the law ought to permit her a life-saving abortion. From the start, we see how her case became a national and then international referendum on the abortion ban. From observing this clash, we understand abortion laws to have a symbolic importance that distinguishes them from ordinary crimes, such as robbery.

Beatriz Files Her Petition

Once Beatriz's doctors refused to terminate her pregnancy, Beatriz's lawyers took two actions. First, they filed a petition with the Salvadoran Supreme Court, seeking a court-ordered abortion for Beatriz. At the time, she was just over four months pregnant. The court took twelve days to respond to her petition.

In the meantime, her lawyers launched a full-scale media campaign. They began by contacting the country's Ministry of Health, the government agency charged with overseeing health care and setting policies for the country's public hospitals, which treat the vast majority of the population. After reviewing Beatriz's medical record, the ministry posted a summary of Beatriz's case on its website, and the minister of health herself gave a statement to the press publicly urging the Supreme Court to permit Beatriz's doctors to interrupt the pregnancy on the grounds that it was the only way to safeguard Beatriz's life.[7]

When the Ministry of Health released its summary of Beatriz's case, along with its recommendation that she be allowed to terminate her pregnancy, her case became a public affair, and Beatriz found herself at the center of an international uproar over abortion. Within a day of filing her petition with the Supreme Court, international organizations from the United Nations to Amnesty International issued statements supporting Beatriz's right to end her pregnancy.

In El Salvador, advocates weighed in on both sides of the debate. Local newspapers issued editorials decrying the ministry's position and urging the court to deny Beatriz's petition. Official organizations such as the Office on Human Rights, with leaders appointed by the left-leaning government, joined the Ministry of Health in calling for the state to permit Beatriz to terminate her pregnancy. They were countered by a coalition of more than fifty groups that joined forces to form the Organization for the Family, whose leaders warned that the case was being used to legalize abortion.[8]

In spite of efforts to conceal Beatriz's identity, journalists found both her mother's house and the two-room home she shared with her

husband and his parents. Television cameras camped outside both loca-
tions, and newscasters harassed her mother in order to get her opinion
on the case.[9] Beatriz, her son, and her husband went into hiding, taking
shelter in a village on the other side of the country, at the home of one
of her lawyer's friends.

Beatriz's Petition Is Referred to the IML

Twelve days after she filed her petition, the Supreme Court agreed to
hear Beatriz's case. The first step in the Supreme Court's evaluation was
to refer her case to the Instituto de Medicina Legal (IML). There's no
US equivalent to the IML, but such institutes are relatively common in
Latin America, where they operate as independent bureaus that com-
bine data collection (e.g., tracking vital statistics and issuing birth and
death certificates) and conduct research or investigations at the behest
of the government.[10]

Rather than simply permitting each side to present medical experts,
the Salvadoran Supreme Court asked the IML to render an independent
expert opinion as to whether Beatriz needed an abortion to save her
life. As a government agency, the IML employs a handful of doctors to
advise it on simple cases. It also has the capacity to call witnesses, such
as Beatriz, and to seek input from additional experts as needed.

"The job of the IML," its director, Dr. Jose Miguel Fortin Magana,
later explained to me, "was not to advise the Supreme Court on whether
to permit the abortion. Instead, our job was simply to answer two questions: one, is Beatriz in imminent danger of dying, and two, is it the
case that terminating the pregnancy is the only treatment that will save
her life?"[11]

A bit of background will help explain how Fortin Magana conducted the inquiry into Beatriz's petition. Unlike the Ministry of Health,
in which all top administrative posts are appointed by the president and
the controlling political party, the IML is considered an independent
government agency, offering support on issues of fact and science. Because these issues are framed as apolitical, rather than conceived of as

policy driven, the director and staff serve indefinite terms of office. They may be appointed by a given president when a vacancy arises, but the expectation is that the director will serve an indefinite term.

At the time of Beatriz's petition, IML director Fortin Magana was a longtime member of the conservative political party, ARENA. By contrast, the president and the head of the Ministry of Health were members of the opposing liberal political party, Farabundo Martí National Liberation Front (FMLN). These parties are not simply political opponents, at least not by US standards. From 1980 to 1992, El Salvador was torn by a civil war in which members of ARENA and FMLN were on opposing sides. Tens of thousands were killed.[12]

Against that political backdrop, consider Fortin Magana's description of the experts appointed to evaluate Beatriz's request. In order to answer the questions of whether Beatriz was dying and whether she could be saved only by having an abortion, Fortin Magana assembled a panel of experts. He said:

> We went to the president of the country's leading medical school and he helped us identify experts. Then we brought in the presidents of the national associations of nephrology, rheumatology, and medical ethics. We didn't know them before.
>
> The Instituto de Medicina Legal brought with it the head of forensic medicine, who is an evangelical, the head of strategic development, who is a Mason, and like myself, a psychiatrist and a Catholic. We didn't need to include experts in obstetrics and gynecology, because the Instituto de Medicina Legal already has these experts on our staff. We only called for the experts we didn't already have.

Two puzzling things stand out in the assemblage of experts who made up the IML's panel. First, there was no one who specialized in high-risk pregnancy. One would expect to find an obstetrician with such expertise on the panel, as this is the branch of the medical profession best qualified to assess the very questions the Supreme Court put to the IML: was Beatriz's condition life-threatening, and was abortion the only way to save her life? The second puzzle was Fortin Magana's emphasis on religious diversity among his experts. Why did he think it important that the experts included Catholics, Masons, and evangelicals? Both of these puzzles indicate how the politics of abortion shaped the legal proceedings in Beatriz's case.

Let me discuss the second puzzle first. Although El Salvador is a democracy, it is also a country in which the vast majority of citizens are religious. Regional studies show that over 90 percent of people in Central America identify as Christians.[13] In El Salvador, the Catholic Church remains the predominant religious organization, with approximately 50 percent of Salvadorans calling themselves Catholic. But the past several decades have witnessed a surge in the popularity of evangelical Christianity, and today, as many as 40 percent of Salvadorans call themselves evangelicals.[14]

By recruiting experts from a variety of religious backgrounds, Fortin Magana was assuring the public of the legitimacy of his process. He listed the participants' religious affiliations to show he had taken steps to safeguard the process against the bias that might come if the experts all reflected a single religious perspective.

Given his attention to concerns about religious diversity, how could it have seemed fair to exclude the country's best experts on managing high-risk pregnancy? In terms of medical expertise, Fortin Magana's panel was limited, at best. As one of Beatriz's doctors later decried: "His experts were a forensic specialist in rape, an ordinary gynecologist, and himself—a psychiatrist—plus some generalists from the medical school. What sort of opinion can a nephrologist [a doctor who treats kidney disease] have on managing pregnancy in a patient with lupus?"[15]

From Fortin Magana's perspective, though, the country's leading high-risk obstetricians were not neutral experts. After the Ministry of Health published Beatriz's case on its website, El Salvador's Association of Obstetricians and Gynecologists sought permission to review Beatriz's full medical record. Shortly after its review, the association, which represents the country's small cadre of experts in treating high-risk pregnancy, went on record by publishing an opinion supporting Beatriz's petition to terminate her pregnancy.[16]

Thus, as Fortin Magana saw things, by the time the IML began to assemble its panel, the country's high-risk obstetricians were no longer neutral. They had already announced their decision about whether Beatriz's life was at risk, about whether she truly needed an abortion.

It is easy for me to slip into cynicism at this point, and to conclude that Fortin Magana, who favored the ban, excluded these medical experts because he knew they'd vote to support an abortion. And perhaps I'd be right in that Fortin Magana's support for the law may well have motivated him to find experts whose views aligned with his own.

But it's also possible to see his actions as an effort to ensure an unbiased audience for Beatriz's evaluation. In announcing their support for Beatriz's right to an abortion, these experts essentially declared they had already made up their minds. Before they met with the other experts, collectively reviewed her medical record, and evaluated her in person, they had already answered the two questions the IML was tasked with reviewing for the Supreme Court: "One, is Beatriz in imminent danger of dying and, two, is it the case that terminating the pregnancy is the only treatment that will save her life?" It was as if they'd decided the case before it was even tried.

When that happens here in the US legal system—as when a judge gives an opinion on a case that is currently or soon to be tried before her—we demand that the judge recuse herself. We worry that a judge who's already made up her mind will not give both sides a fair hearing.

In Beatriz's case, if the doctors already supported her right to abort on the grounds that this pregnancy was life threatening, then it was obvious how they would answer the court's narrower questions about imminent danger of dying and treatment alternatives.

So it is that, before we even lift the curtain on the first of Beatriz's legal hearings, we can see how the politics of abortion permeated not only the realm of law, but also that of science.

The Instituto de Medicina Legal Evaluates Beatriz's Petition

The IML panel took almost six weeks to review Beatriz's medical record. It pored over hundreds of pages describing her first pregnancy, the health crisis it precipitated, and the successful outcome after an emergency cesarean section delivery. The panel reviewed the tests and examinations pertaining to Beatriz's current pregnancy, and then, on May 3, it summoned Beatriz from the hospital to the IML offices for a physical examination. By that time, she was twenty-three-weeks pregnant.

Fortin Magana was one of three evaluating physicians. Because the hearing happened behind closed doors, all I know comes from what Beatriz told me, a year later, when I asked her to describe it:

> There were three doctors. I didn't know their names. They didn't make me undress. They just checked my face and my hands, looked at the marks on my skin. And listened to my breath. They asked about my childhood and made me do some drawings. I guess they wanted to see if I was OK in my head. Maybe they thought I was crazy because of what I wanted to do.

On May 8, Fortin Magana announced the decision on behalf of the IML. It found that Beatriz was stable and, as such, there was no need to terminate the pregnancy.[17]

"Terminating the pregnancy was not necessary," Fortin Magana told me, "nor would it remedy her chronic illness":

> Our conclusion was unanimous; we advocated conservative treatment. We never said, as was reported throughout the world, that her life wasn't important or shouldn't be saved. On the contrary, we specifically said she could terminate the pregnancy if her symptoms worsened

and her life was in danger. The doctors could put the infant in an incubator and if God wants, it will live, and if God doesn't want, it will die. But we weren't leaving Beatriz in danger of dying.[18]

After the IML's May 8 ruling, the Salvadoran Supreme Court agreed to hear arguments from both sides of Beatriz's case a week later, on May 15. During that week, her supporters mounted a publicity campaign, using political connections, social media, and the international press to plead her case. The political firestorm that ensued reminds us of the extent to which Beatriz's case became a referendum on abortion. It shows how both sides understood the stakes and gives us a sense of the pressures the case placed on the Supreme Court.

Shortly after the IML released its report finding that Beatriz was stable, Salvadoran minister of health Dr. Maria Isabel Rodriguez gave a public interview condemning the report. In it, she described Beatriz's medical condition in vivid detail and made the case for abortion, telling the press that therapeutic abortion was the only "viable and just solution," and that Fortin Magana's declarations were "crude and rude."[19]

President Mauricio Funes, who had not addressed the subject of abortion in the first four years of his five-year presidency, announced his belief that Beatriz had the right to make decisions about her own life.[20]

Beatriz's supporters filmed her, the image cropped to show only her puffy hands, blotchy and red from the lupus, folded over her obviously pregnant belly.

"I want to live," she said quietly. "I beg from my heart that you let me."

The video went viral, circulated by Amnesty International and other social media outlets throughout the world.[21]

At the same time, international pro-life groups such as Human Life International called on El Salvador to hold fast to its opposition to abortion under all circumstances.[22]

Julia Regina de Cardenal, the head of El Salvador's pro-life movement Sí a la Vida and also a columnist for *El Diario de Hoy*, one of the country's two leading newspapers, cast the debate over Beatriz as an assault on Salvadoran sovereignty:

> In our country the Constitution defends all human life against the powerful interests of those who manipulate situations like this in order to open the door to the multinational multimillion-dollar abortion industry. The IML uncovered the truth: showing that Beatriz is stable, that she can continue her pregnancy, that medical intervention will be possible as soon as any complication arises, in spite of the false declarations of pro-abortion groups, the Ministry of Health and international organizations, among others. We await the apologies of the United Nations, the International Court of Human Rights, the Organization of American States and Amnesty International for having pressured our leaders to commit a crime with grave consequences for Beatriz and her baby.[23]

The Supreme Court Proceedings

On May 15, 2013, the Supreme Court held a closed-door hearing. Beatriz arrived in an ambulance, accompanied by a caravan of trucks and cars bearing her doctors, representatives of the Ministry of Health, expert witnesses, and lawyers. The morning session was devoted to establishing the credentials of experts offered by both sides. The technicalities were strictly enforced. So strictly, in fact, that the court barred the testimony of the defense's key expert on the grounds that he had brought only a copy, rather than an original, medical diploma. That expert was world-renowned Brazilian obstetrician Dr. Anibal Faundes, who was to have testified about international standard of care in cases involving lupus during pregnancy. Without his testimony, Beatriz's lawyers lost their strongest testimony regarding the international standard of care that they had hoped to invoke in support of Beatriz's need for an abortion.[24]

After the court heard arguments from both sides, it announced that it would render its decision within fifteen working days.[25] To be sure, the case was a difficult one, forcing the justices to resolve what seemed to be an impasse between the competing rights to life of Beatriz and her fetus. On the one hand, abortion was banned. On the other hand, the Salvadoran constitution guaranteed the same fundamental rights to every person, including those not yet born. Still, fifteen days was a long time, and Beatriz's health status was growing increasingly precarious.

On May 29, 2013, the Supreme Court announced its opinion. In it, the court rejected Beatriz's petition for an abortion, citing the IML's conclusion that Beatriz's right to life was not imperiled: she was receiving treatment according to "medical science," consisting of hospitalization and constant monitoring to ensure that her health remained stable. Therefore, it concluded the state was adequately protecting Beatriz's fundamental rights to health and life.[26]

Key to the opinion is the court's refusal to choose between Beatriz's right to life and that of her fetus. Although the court acknowledged the possibility that, at some point in the future, these rights might come into conflict, it took pains to avoid privileging one life over the other.[27] Instead, it instructed the doctors to follow medical guidelines in determining the opportune moment for any intervention, noting that their decision should be based upon their clinical analysis of the best treatment to secure the lives of both the mother and the fetus.

The Aftermath of the Legal Proceedings

The court's decision placed Beatriz's doctors in what one of them called the "ridiculous" situation of "knowing that her life was going to be imperiled, yet having to wait until it actually was in order to save her."[28] Further complicating Beatriz's medical status was the fact that Beatriz had delivered her first child via a cesarean section delivery. Although vaginal births are possible after cesarean section deliveries, in El Salvador, the risks of uterine rupture and other complications are considered too high. Thus, her doctors knew Beatriz would need a cesarean section, and yet they understood the law as barring them from scheduling one until Beatriz became medically unstable. Of course, once she was medically unstable, the cesarean section would be a complex and risky operation.

Finally, when she was twenty-seven weeks pregnant, Beatriz began having pre-term contractions. Her doctors knew they couldn't let her risk going into labor. They performed a cesarean section, and Beatriz's baby girl was delivered. Beatriz bled more than normal after the surgery, but she was readily stabilized. Her newborn daughter was placed on life support in an incubator, where she died, five hours after she was born.

UNDERSTANDING THE MEANING AND PURPOSE OF ABORTION BANS: WHAT WE LEARN FROM BEATRIZ'S CASE

Try as I might to see another viewpoint, the outcome in Beatriz's case seemed to me perverse. El Salvador forced Beatriz to wait until her life was in immediate danger before allowing her to terminate her pregnancy. The law increased the chances that she would suffer permanent damage to her vital organs; it forced her to endure months of physical pain and psychological distress. And all for the sake of a fetus that everyone agreed would never survive.

A year after the decision, when it had faded from public view, I went to El Salvador to try to make sense of it all. I found doctors and lawyers on both sides of the conflict who were generous with their time and helped me to understand not only the reasons Beatriz's case unfolded as it did, but also the purpose and significance of the abortion law itself.

The Distinction Between a Life-Threatening Pregnancy and Imminent Risk of Death

One of the most outspoken medical experts in support of the government's position in Beatriz's case petition was Dr. Carlos Mayora. Both during and afterward, he appeared on media outlets throughout El Salvador. An obstetrician in his eighties who'd worked for decades in private practice, Mayora's white-jacket commentary conveyed grandfatherly authority. He gave so many interviews making the case for denying Beatriz's petition to terminate her pregnancy that he became the de facto spokesperson for the opposition.

I was determined to reach out and see whether he would be willing to talk to me about Beatriz's case. After my attempts to reach him by e-mail failed, I screwed up my courage and called his office.

"Dr. Mayora," his gravelly voice announced, when his secretary put through my call.

"Good afternoon," I said, launching into my carefully rehearsed Spanish introduction. "I'm a law professor from California. I'm researching the well-known case of Beatriz and I'm coming to El Salvador in a few weeks and was wondering whether you might be willing to let me interview you."

"*Bueno*," he answered. "Why don't you send me a description of your study?"

He had understood me. I was amazed and thrilled.

"Certainly, and I have explained it all in Spanish. I speak well in person, but I get nervous on the telephone, so I would love to send you the details. What is your e-mail address?"

"Well, that's not necessary. You can send it to my office."

"Send it by mail to El Salvador? Are you sure? Is there someone else I could e-mail it to?"

"That's not necessary. Just send it to me."

When I got to his office, I saw my papers had arrived, in spite of my doubts about the reliability of the Salvadoran postal system. Mayora had also printed out a tall stack of my articles. As I offered my thanks for agreeing to meet with me, he motioned to them, saying, "See, we know who you are," his face crinkling into a wide smile.

He'd invited his friend Delmer Rodriguez, a constitutional law professor from the Superior School of Economics and Business, to join us. In addition to a brightly painted, wooden business-card holder, Rodriguez gave me a pocket-sized copy of the Salvadoran constitution.

"Look at *Article I*," Rodriguez pointed out, opening the small book. "It's written here: life begins at conception. It's a human being. We put it there in 1998 because it's the most important part of our law—protecting human life."

"But it's not simply a legal concept; it's a scientific fact," added Mayora, lifting a heavy volume from the books on his shelf. "It's here in *Williams Obstetrics*. It's an American book. Are you familiar with it? This one is in Spanish, of course, from 2008. But it says here, 'There's a unique DNA.' The fetus is totally distinct from the moment of conception. It's an individual and the law signifies this fact."

I had encountered the "separate DNA" argument before, when talking with pro-life advocates in the United States. As they see it, the fact that a fetus has its own chromosomal makeup proves that it is a separate individual. If it is a separate individual, it deserves the same rights as does any other member of the human community. Its location inside of its mother in no way diminishes its humanity.

I understand their argument. I even agree with them that the fetus is in a sense "alive." But I reject their conclusion that, because a fetus has a unique genetic makeup, abortion is always wrong.

In my religious tradition, until a baby is born alive, it is not considered a separate human being. We don't treat fetuses like other human beings. For example, although there is grief when a woman loses a pregnancy, we don't have funerals or engage in traditional mourning practices for miscarried fetuses. My sense is that the same holds true for most other religions. So to my way of thinking, location matters: the fetus is alive and has a unique DNA, but until it is born, it is not a separate human being.

In Beatriz's case, her fetus never would survive outside her body. In the meantime, its location inside her body posed a serious threat to her life.

"What I want to know," I asked Mayora, "is why, if the mother's life is in danger, it should be illegal to terminate the pregnancy? Not with the intention of killing the fetus, but in the double-effect sense. You know, where the goal is to save her life, but the only way to do so is to end the pregnancy."

I had learned about the Catholic doctrine of double-effect years ago, when teaching medical ethics at a Catholic hospital in Chicago. In the context of abortion, this doctrine permits an exception to the general religious prohibition against abortion when the act is intended to save the mother's life. In this case, because the goal is to save the mother's life, the abortion has the double-effect of saving her life—a moral good—and the negative, but unwanted, effect of ending the fetus's life.[29] The doctrine seemed to me tailor-made for a case like this.

But Mayora did not want to discuss Catholic ethics. Instead, he was interested in the way Beatriz's case was being used to advocate for an exception to the abortion ban.

"Her doctors found that the fetus lacked a brain, which is totally incompatible with life. It looked like a worm. In my judgment, the doctors thought in good faith that this girl was carrying a fetus that couldn't survive," he said.

But he believed her supporters were exaggerating Beatriz's condition in order to get the state to make an exception to its abortion ban:

> Her lawyers presented Beatriz's case very dramatically. But she already had had a child who survived. And then she got pregnant again, in spite of the fact that the doctors had warned her to take precautions against pregnancy. She got pregnant again, and had been going to and from her doctors' appointments by herself. She was living at home, seventy-five miles from San Salvador, but coming every week by public bus to her prenatal appointments. So she was healthy, you see?
>
> Then, the advocates, a group of radical feminists, took her away to a shelter of American women. Even though we, as an organization, offered her a private lodging. The feminist group said "no." They had her isolated there, basically deprived her of her liberty, and made her an emblematic case. To make a law in favor of abortion.

How can I describe Mayora so that you'll understand why I failed to interrupt to press him for clearer answers? Surely a trained journalist or anthropologist would have managed to get to the heart of the matter. His crinkled eyes were blue, his hands enormous. The smile lines so deep they seemed sculpted. When he spoke of God, his deep voice grew quiet.

I knew the advocates. They were not Americans, but Salvadorans. They had taken Beatriz into hiding in order to escape the media frenzy.

I still couldn't understand why, if he agreed both that Beatriz's fetus was doomed and that it was only a matter of time until the pregnancy placed her life in danger, he nonetheless supported making her wait before terminating it.

When I asked him why she needed to wait, Mayora responded that, at the time of her petition to the Supreme Court for an abortion, Beatriz's medical condition was stable. And at the same time, her fetus was alive, its heart was beating, and it was growing day by day. Unless and until the pregnancy posed an "imminent threat" to Beatriz's life, it was wrong to kill the fetus.

Later, when I described this part of my conversation to Dr. Jorge Ramirez, the chief assistant to the minister of health, he bristled: "Ask them if those who survived the 9/11 attack on the Twin Towers were never in danger. Because they survived? They say things that are indefensible."[30]

I did ask Mayora at least one direct question, though: "If she'd really been dying, would you have supported her desire to terminate her pregnancy?"

And he answered, "Yes."

I managed a lawyerly follow-up: "Have you ever treated a woman whose life was in danger as a result of her pregnancy?"

"I worked for thirty-five years at Social Security—the country's second-largest public hospital system, and also in the largest one, La Maternidad," he answered. "I've been a doctor for fifty-five years. I believe medicine has grown in its capacity to respond to pregnancy-related problems. And in this case, when the Instituto de Medicina Legal evaluated Beatriz, it saw she wasn't dying; that it had been a complete exaggeration."

The Law of Self-Defense and Beatriz's Life-Threatening Pregnancy

Long after the conversation with Mayora and Rodriguez, after meeting Fortin Magana and after parsing the Supreme Court's opinion, I came to see how El Salvador interpreted the law of self-defense in Beatriz's case. I was so distracted by the politics of the case—by the assertions of bad faith on both sides—that I forgot to pay attention to the law that ultimately permitted Beatriz's doctors to interrupt her pregnancy.

The legal principle of self-defense was evident in Mayora's focus on whether Beatriz was dying. Because the fetus was considered as much a human being as was Beatriz, a justification for taking its life would arise only if and when the fetus posed an imminent threat to Beatriz's life.

By relying on the law of self-defense, El Salvador's decision permitted doctors to save Beatriz's life without in any way diminishing the moral status or the legal rights of her fetus. In El Salvador, after Beatriz's case, life still begins at conception and abortion is still completely banned.

Self-defense is an ancient legal principle, as much a part of US law as it is a part of El Salvador's. The conventional definition provides:

> One who is not the aggressor in an encounter is justified in using a reasonable amount of force against his adversary where he reasonably believes (a) that he is in immediate danger of unlawful bodily harm from his adversary and (b) that the use of such force is necessary to avoid this danger.[31]

It doesn't take a law degree to spot the slippery terms in this definition. Who's an *adversary*? What's *immediate danger*? And what's *unlawful bodily harm*?

El Salvador answered these questions in Beatriz's case by acknowledging that the fetus would become an adversary at the point where

Beatriz's doctors could no longer stabilize her condition. At that point, when the risk of death was imminent, Beatriz's fundamental rights to health and life would be deemed imperiled.[32] As such, her doctors would be justified in interrupting the pregnancy, even if they killed the fetus in the process. Critically, the intention in intervening would be to save Beatriz's life, rather than to kill the fetus. Indeed, the opinion directed them to employ all means of saving the baby's life.[33]

Had Beatriz's case arisen here in the United States, the requirement of imminence might not have been interpreted so strictly. "The proper inquiry," says one leading commentator, "is not the immediacy of the threat but the immediacy of the response necessary in defense. If a threatened harm is such that it cannot be avoided if the intended victim waits until the last moment, the principle of self-defense must permit him to act earlier—as early as is required to defend himself effectively."[34]

The Salvadoran Supreme Court's opinion arguably allowed this option of early intervention to Beatriz's doctors. The court said that it was up to her doctors to determine the precise moment when medical protocols demanded intervention.[35] But because the opinion added that those protocols ought to be based upon evidence of "real and immediate risk to the life of the pregnant mother," and because the risk of a miscalculation on their part meant possible criminal sanctions, Beatriz's doctors elected to wait until her life hung in the balance.

My hunch is that the Supreme Court struggled when applying the law of self-defense to a fetus. How odd to cast the fetus as an assailant against whom deadly force is justified. Unlike conventional adversaries, the fetus doesn't do or intend anything toward its mother.

Perhaps, too, the court was moved, in narrowing the scope of self-defense, by a sense that Beatriz was partly to blame for her predicament. After all, Beatriz became pregnant again, against medical advice, even though her first pregnancy almost killed her.[36] My conversations with Mayora, Rodriguez, and Fortin Magana did not go deep enough to explore the possibility that they blamed Beatriz for her situation, but all mentioned the fact that she'd gotten pregnant a second time, in spite of knowing its risk to her health.

The way they invoked her choice to get pregnant a second time reminded me of a familiar undercurrent in our debate over legalized abortion here in the United States: the idea that some women are more deserving of an abortion than others. It's surprisingly common for those who would ban abortion to support exceptions in cases of rape and incest. The reasoning seems to be that these women had pregnancy forced on them when they were raped. Because they did not choose to have sex, they should not be forced to carry a pregnancy, regardless of the humanity of the developing fetus. I could spend pages exploring what's wrong with the assumption that, by having sex, a woman waives her fundamental rights to protect her own health and safety, should she become pregnant.

But in Beatriz's case, such debates are unnecessary. Because, as you'll see momentarily, Beatriz did not choose to become pregnant. Nor did she describe the sex leading to her pregnancy as voluntary.

In the media and in the courtroom, Beatriz's case was understood as a challenge to El Salvador's abortion ban. But in order to take the true measure of the ban, so that we understand how much and how little laws governing abortion matter, we need to understand Beatriz as a human being, rather than merely an abstraction.

BEATRIZ'S STORY

Arranging to meet Beatriz was easy. Having spent four years researching abortion in El Salvador, I already knew many key players in Beatriz's case. At 6 a.m., one June morning in 2014, I set out from San Salvador with Sara Garcia, one of the activists who'd advocated on her behalf.

It took two and a half hours to get from the capital to the dirt road turnoff to La Gloria (pseudonym). It took another forty-five minutes to find the home of Beatriz's mother, less than a mile away. The dirt road was muddy with the previous night's rains. We traveled slowly, trying to stay in the ruts. A herd of bony cows moved slowly in front of us. A man on horseback rode behind them, randomly whipping the stragglers so that they lumbered to one side or the other, without ever clearing the street.

The village of La Gloria has only one road. There were no signs or numbers, but Garcia didn't want to ask directions of the occasional neighbors for fear of calling attention to Beatriz's family. Beatriz and her son had moved from the house of her husband's parents and were staying with her mother, Delmy, for a while.

Delmy's high voice came over Garcia's cell phone, guiding us to a bumpy lane that angled off the main road, then opened onto a clearing with two brightly painted churches and, farther down, five or six cinder-block houses. Finally, we saw her waving to us from across a muddy yard scattered with brick stepping-stones. Chickens patrolled the yard, clucking as we passed under a wire clothesline strung from an electricity pole.

Beatriz waited in the doorway's shadow, her eyes as enormous as a baby's. Two impossibly small kittens played by her feet.

"Come in, come in," Delmy said, with hugs and a kiss on the cheek.

My eyes adjusted to the dim room. Beatriz sat on one of the two red plastic lawn chairs, inviting Garcia and me to sit in the two hammocks that crisscrossed the room. Her mother unpacked the bag of groceries—rice, beans, corn flour, cookies, and tampons—that we'd brought from the "super" market in Zacatecoluca, the nearest town. I tried to engage Claudio, Beatriz's two-and-a-half-year-old son, who was playing ball with a rectangular blow-up pillow. He kicked it around the room, until it went under the bed. He cried until Beatriz got up and coaxed it out with a broken umbrella. He'd hit his head some time ago on the bed's metal underside and wouldn't go under himself. After the fourth or fifth time, Beatriz ignored his crying and left the pillow ball under the bed.

Claudio brought out his other toy, a plastic bowl in which he carried three ketchup packets. While Garcia tried getting him to say "one, two, three," Beatriz, Delmy, and I chatted about children, theirs and mine. Delmy couldn't believe that, at fifty-three, I wasn't yet a grandmother. She's forty-one and already has several grandchildren.

As the sun angled slowly into their home, Beatriz's sixteen-year-old sister arrived, carrying her eight-month-old son. Delmy gave her three dollars and sent her to the neighbor's stand to buy Coca-Cola and some *pupusas*. She stayed and chatted for a while when she returned, then kissed her mother good-bye and left. Later, Beatriz's fourteen-year-old sister emerged from behind the curtain that separated the small bedroom in the back from the house's main room where we sat. She poured water over herself from a bucket in the outdoor basin, pulled on white knee socks, and then left for her three-hour school day. Still later, Beatriz's eighteen-year-old brother arrived, carrying a clear plastic bag filled with scores of baby tilapia. He was hoping to raise them in the gray tub next to the latrine and maybe sell them one day.

Beatriz leaned forward as I spoke, smiling as she got used to my accent. I tried sitting up in the hammock to create a lap for one of the kittens, and suddenly flipped over and fell onto the floor. Even Claudio stopped whining, and after a stunned moment, we all laughed. I dusted myself off—the cement floor was covered with a persistent layer of crisp gold sand, although we were miles from the beach—and took a seat in one of the chairs.

Beatriz was ready to tell me her story.

I already knew most of it. Her doctors had described the painful lupus sores, red and itchy, that began spreading all over her body. The way pregnancy escalated her disease, the trip to the experts in San Salvador, the ultrasound with its terrible news about the fetus. And everyone knew about the ensuing legal battle.

What caught me by surprise was not the story she told, but Beatriz herself. She'd seemed entirely passive in the public story told about her case—a person to whom things had happened. Lupus. A fetus with no brain. A girl who got pregnant a second time, in spite of her doctors' warnings. In person, though, she was not so much passive as she was trapped.

The truth is that Beatriz *chose* not to get sterilized after her first child, Claudio, was born. At first it wasn't clear whether Claudio would survive; he'd been delivered so early. She didn't get sterilized then because she wanted the chance to have a child, in case Claudio died. Later, when Claudio came home, and it became clear that he wasn't developing normally, her reasons for not getting sterilized grew more complicated.

The truth is that her life was almost impossibly difficult before she became pregnant a second time.

At her mother's home, she and Claudio slept in the front room on a thin foam mattress over a sagging metal frame. There was no money for diapers, so she awakened night after night in a puddle of urine. Claudio didn't speak and seemed unable to understand even basic commands. There were four other people sharing the two-room living space.

Beatriz had left school at age fourteen. She'd never held a job, and no one she knew earned a regular income. And she was sick. Her lupus was so advanced that medications barely controlled her blood pressure. She was weak, easily tired, and at constant risk of stroke.

There was no marked path, no clear way in which Beatriz could have stepped out of the life she was living and into one in which she had good options. Instead, she moved back and forth between her mother's home and her in-laws' home every few weeks.

She moved because her husband beat her. Inside of the cinder-block house he shared with his parents, he hit her. Then she would leave him, taking Claudio with her. They would make up. She would move back. He would beat her again.

She told me about his violence in passing, when I asked how she felt, now that her case was over and done with.

"I feel guilty," she said. "I know it wasn't my fault that the baby died. But we were guilty for not having taken precautions."

"You feel guilty for having gotten pregnant?" I asked.

"He didn't take care," she said, speaking softly. "We always have problems between us, so . . ."

Beatriz's voice trailed off, and I thought perhaps I needed to move on. But then she continued, "One day we fought. He knew that I couldn't have children, but he told me that he wanted me to get pregnant anyhow, even though he knew what could happen. So he wouldn't use a condom."

We had been talking for hours by this point. I didn't know what to say. Telling her that she'd been raped, that getting pregnant wasn't her fault, wouldn't change how she felt. And my hunch was that, in her mind, she felt guilty because she didn't get sterilized, even though she knew a second pregnancy might kill her. She knew what was at stake: she did not get sterilized because she feared that, if she did, she would lose her husband.

Claudio stood in the doorway crying. Pee ran down his leg. Beatriz got up from the chair, reached for some newspaper from a stack near the door, and laid it on the wet spot.

"Does it feel like it was a long time ago, when we talk about what happened?" I asked, hoping the present was so distracting that it might help her to forget the past.

"No, it feels like it's only a few days ago. It's not the past."

Beatriz was crying in earnest now, but she had raised her eyes and was looking straight at me.

"It's made me want to be somewhere else. Like, I always want to be with my mother when I'm with my husband. And then I want to be with my husband when I'm with my mother. Sometimes, I feel desperate in all of my body, and I don't want to be alive. But my mom tells me that I have to fight for the child that I have. God still wants me to be here, and my son needs me."

CONCLUSION

At some point on the journey home, it occurred to me how little difference it would have made had Beatriz been granted an abortion at fourteen weeks. Of course, it would have been better for her not to have lain in the hospital for months, worrying about her son, her mother, her husband, and the possibility that she would die.

But an early abortion, like the later induced delivery, would have offered no permanent relief from the things that made her life hard. Beatriz's case meant more to the war over abortion than the abortion meant to Beatriz.

To those who oppose the abortion ban, Beatriz's case offered the perfect challenge to the ban's legitimacy. Making an exception to permit Beatriz an abortion—whether because the fetus lacked a brain, or because her life was at risk, or both—would amount to an admission that the ban went too far. If Beatriz was allowed to end her pregnancy, there would be precedent for favoring a mother's rights over those of her fetus. Her case would be the first of many.

Those who supported the abortion ban understood this threat. This case was not about their conviction that Beatriz's fetus was viable or could, by some miracle, survive. Mayora, the leading spokesperson in support of denying Beatriz an abortion, had said, "It looked like a worm," and made no pretense about its chances for life.

But they understood the risk of making an exception in Beatriz's case.

In the end, Beatriz's case became a high-stakes game, played to a draw. Beatriz survived. But so did the abortion ban.

I understand both sides. If a fetus or, for that matter, a zygote is a full member of the human community, the battle over abortion must be fought in an all-or-nothing manner.[37] The law banning abortion is simply the legal embodiment of a moral truth. It is a declaration of membership in the human species.

Using the law to make moral declarations is not unusual. It's what legal theorists call the "expressive function" of the law.[38] We use the law to tell us something about ourselves—who we are and what we value.

Think of laws against prostitution, flag-burning, or organ-selling. To the extent one supports these laws, it's often for reasons beyond or even aside from a belief that the law will prevent the crime from happening. Instead, we look to the law as a way of proclaiming moral boundaries. Supporters use the law to testify to a shared moral vision.

But valuing a law because of the statement it makes does not mean that one doesn't care about its impact. Consequences matter. So, for example, if evidence showed that a law against selling human organs had the effect of intensifying the exploitation and misery of the relevant vulnerable populations, one might reconsider his or her support for that law.

Professor Cass Sunstein, in his leading work on the expressive function of law, suggests that the biggest challenge to symbolic laws arises when "the effects of such laws seem bad or ambiguous, even by reference to the values held by their supporters."[39] Only a fanatic, he reasons, would completely ignore the law's impact on the norms and values it aims to promote.[40]

Until I began my travels in El Salvador, I did not fully appreciate the moral position that life begins at conception, and the ways in which that moral conviction might lead inexorably to supporting a complete ban on abortion. But as Sunstein notes, the ultimate test of a law's legitimacy, even of a law intended primarily to make a symbolic statement, lies in its consequences.

It is not enough to assert that a law's consequence is good simply because it makes a good statement. That circularity is a fanatic's position.

Beatriz's case was, by all accounts, extraordinary. In the next chapter, we turn to the subject of ordinary abortions and of the measurable consequences of El Salvador's endeavor to outlaw them.

TWO

ASSESSING THE IMPACT OF EL SALVADOR'S ABORTION BAN

In 1998, El Salvador passed a law banning abortion under all circumstances.[1] Until that point, abortion was illegal except in cases involving risks to maternal life, severe fetal anomaly, and rape or incest. Since then, El Salvador has worked to enforce its ban, mounting an intensive effort to identify and prosecute those who violate the law. If we're hoping to understand what happens when abortion is banned, El Salvador is the perfect place to study.

Regardless of whether one favors or opposes the abortion ban, it is vital that we assess the law's impact. Recall Cass Sunstein's observation at the end of the last chapter that a law cannot be justified merely because one likes its message. Even if we like the message of the law, it is valid only to the extent that it produces results that are consistent with its message.

So what happened when abortion was outlawed in El Salvador? The evidence shows us that three things occurred: (1) abortion remained commonplace and rates did not drop even though it was illegal; (2) doctors become involved in law enforcement; and (3) innocent women were accused and convicted of abortion-related crimes. These three systems—the black market, health care, and criminal justice—all yield measurable consequences of the ban on abortion. And, as I explain below, in spite of the vast differences between El Salvador and the United States, there is good reason to expect that the United States would experience each of these three consequences were it to outlaw abortion.

ABORTIONS STILL HAPPEN

Perhaps the most surprising thing about banning abortion is what doesn't happen when abortion becomes a crime. Abortion does not go away. Indeed, the rates of abortion in countries with the most restrictive abortion laws are higher.[2]

This is true in El Salvador: by the Salvadoran government's own measure, there are tens of thousands of illegal abortions every year.[3] Indeed, the rate of abortion in countries with restrictive abortion laws far exceeds that of countries with far more liberal laws, such as the United States.[4]

The correlation of high abortion rates and restrictive abortion laws does not mean that abortion bans *cause* more women to have abortions. Any number of factors might cause these two things—abortion bans and high abortion rates—to go together. Perhaps these countries share a religious or cultural discomfort with contraception, as well as abortion. Perhaps it is hard to get contraception. Perhaps there is little sex education.

There is one thing we know for certain: abortion doesn't simply go away when it is made illegal. Because abortions are illegal, it is hard to get a complete picture of how women obtain them in El Salvador. What is clear beyond a doubt is that the advent of abortion drugs has completely altered illegal abortion.

Until recently, abortions were exclusively surgical procedures.[5] Doctors would terminate pregnancies by opening the cervix and suctioning or scraping out the contents of the uterus. Women unable to find or afford a doctor to perform an illegal abortion might try bringing on a miscarriage themselves, for example, by inserting a sharp object into their uterus. Opening the cervix typically is enough to induce a miscarriage, although it carries with it high risks of excessive bleeding and infection.

Historically, these so-called "botched" abortions provided the only proof of the crime of illegal abortion. Coat-hanger abortions, for example, were notorious in pre-*Roe* America, in part because they carried a high risk of perforating a woman's uterus, leaving behind the telltale sign that the woman had deliberately ended her pregnancy.

Beginning in the 1990s, with the advent of abortion drugs, illegal abortion became safer and harder to detect. Taken in the appropriate dose, at the right point in pregnancy, the drug known as Mifeprex or RU-486 (mifepristone is the generic name) will safely end 98 percent of pregnancies.[6] Side effects include excessive bleeding or incomplete abortion, both readily resolved by a visit to a doctor.[7]

Although they are not always safe or effective, especially when taken too late in pregnancy or at the wrong dose, compared with the risks of an illegal surgical abortion, drugs such as RU-486 or Mifeprex have completely altered women's access to illegal abortion.[8] In many countries, women find it easy to buy misoprostol, a drug conventionally used in treating gastric ulcers. It happens to be one of two of the drugs that, together, make up Mifeprex. Taken alone, misoprostol is slightly less safe and less effective than Mifeprex, ending between 75 and 90 percent of first-trimester pregnancies, as opposed to Mifeprex, which ends 98 percent of pregnancies. Still, the side effects of misoprostol, such as heavy bleeding or incomplete abortion, are minimal and easily treated, unlike those associated with incompetently performed surgical abortions.[9]

In El Salvador, and throughout Latin America, women find it easy to access misoprostol via the Internet.[10] In Brazil, for example, where abortion is illegal except in cases of rape, threat to maternal life, or anencephaly (where the fetus lacks a brain), abortion drugs play a vital role in the thriving black market. An estimated one in five Brazilian women under age forty has had an abortion.[11] Even in a poor country like El Salvador, almost everyone has a smartphone and, provided they have money and time, can go online to purchase the drugs that will end an unwanted pregnancy.

To be sure, illegal abortion remains risky.[12] Whether they use drugs or other means to terminate their pregnancies, many women experience complications from illegal abortion that necessitate medical attention. In Latin America, complications from illegal abortion constitute the leading cause of mortality in young women.[13]

The inevitability of such complications has led to the second concrete change set in motion by banning abortions: doctors become entangled in the law enforcement process.

DOCTORS AND THE PROBLEM OF DETECTING ABORTION

If the first thing that happened when El Salvador banned abortion was the proliferation of illegal, black-market abortions, the second thing that happened was that doctors were enlisted in the law enforcement effort. The overwhelming majority of abortion cases in El Salvador begin in the hospital, with a doctor's hunch that his or her patient has broken the law.

In 1998, Salvadoran government officials charged with implementing the newly passed abortion ban reached out to doctors to encourage them to report patients they suspected of terminating their pregnancies. Dr. Alejandro Guidos, former president of the El Salvadoran Association of Obstetricians and Gynecologists, described the state's approach. He told me, "Officials from the Fiscalia [the state prosecutors] went to the hospitals, advising doctors that they had a legal obligation to report women suspected of terminating their pregnancies. And the hospital directors supported the obligation to report. They collaborated."[14]

The push to enlist doctors in enforcing the abortion law succeeded. A 2006 survey of practicing obstetricians found that more than half (56 percent) of respondents reported having been involved in notifying legal authorities about a suspected unlawful abortion.[15]

Inevitably, a country seeking to enforce laws against abortion will seek doctors' collaboration. Women must turn to doctors when an illegal abortion goes wrong. Doctors are therefore in the best position to spot the crime.

But there are serious problems with using doctors to enforce abortion laws. In reporting their patients, doctors break the law and violate the oldest of ethical principles—patient confidentiality. Furthermore, in the vast majority of cases, doctors cannot tell whether a woman has had an abortion or simply a miscarriage. Thus, their reports are based on hunches, rather than on medical evidence.

Law, Ethics, and Doctors' Reports to Police

The obligation of safeguarding a patient's secrets is ancient. For over twenty-four hundred years, medical doctors have embraced the precepts articulated in the Hippocratic oath.[16] Recited at medical school graduations worldwide, one of the oath's central tenets is the following pledge: "Whatever I see or hear in the lives of my patients, whether in connection with my professional practice or not, which ought not to be spoken of outside, I will keep secret, as considering all such things to be private."[17]

This principle is based in part on policy considerations. Confidentiality is essential to creating a solid doctor-patient relationship, dedicated to promoting the health and life of the patient. Doctors routinely treat patients whom they suspect or even know to have broken the law. The medical profession long has been clear that its job is to heal, rather than to work as agents of the police.

In El Salvador, as in other countries, including the United States, the ethical obligation of confidentiality has been enacted into law; it is illegal to share patient information.[18] A doctor who reveals her patients' medical information commits both a civil wrong, for which a patient might sue, and a crime, punishable by imprisonment and the suspension of the doctor's medical license.[19]

Regardless of these ethical and legal precepts, it's easy to understand why a doctor might struggle when encountering evidence of an illegal abortion. If you view abortion as the taking of a life, you might be willing to call the police, even if it means violating the norms and laws governing confidentiality.

Salvadoran law supports such breaches of confidentiality by requiring doctors to report suspected crimes to the state.[20] Because abortion is a "criminal act," this requirement could be construed to mean that providers must report cases of unlawful abortion to police. Plainly, this was the interpretation the Salvadoran officials meant to convey when they toured hospitals in 1998.

Legally, though, they were wrong. The law explicitly excuses doctors from this duty when the information is acquired in the course of a confidential doctor-patient relationship. The law states that "[d]octors, pharmacists, nurses and other health professionals must report unlawful criminal acts that they become aware of in the context of their professional relationship, *unless the information they acquire is protected under the terms of professional secrecy.*"[21]

There is no conflict under the law, then. Doctors are required to maintain patient confidentiality.

Still, when the state sends prosecutors to inform hospital personnel of the need to report patients they suspect of having abortions, one can understand why doctors might comply. What happened next was both inevitable and deeply troubling.

The Diagnostic Challenge: Distinguishing Abortion from Miscarriage

It's almost always impossible, even for doctors, to tell whether a woman has had an abortion or instead simply suffered a common spontaneous miscarriage. Indeed, miscarriage is so common an occurrence that, in Spanish, there is no difference between the word for miscarriage and the word for abortion. Any interruption of pregnancy is termed an *aborto*. Although women in El Salvador, like women in the United States, tend not to speak openly about losing a pregnancy to miscarriage, when they do so, they say they've had an *aborto*. There is no other way to describe their loss.

Throughout the world, as many as one in four pregnancies ends in spontaneous miscarriage.[22] Miscarriage most often happens early in pregnancy—within the first twelve weeks. A woman having a miscarriage typically experiences what feels like a heavier period than normal, perhaps passing more blood and some blood clots, along with whatever fetal tissue remained in her uterus after the fetus stopped developing.[23] A woman might seek medical care following an early miscarriage, in response to heavy bleeding or cramping, or because of the risk that her body hasn't expelled all the fetal tissue.

Herein lies the inevitable challenge for abortion law enforcement: in the absence of physical evidence such as trauma to the uterus, there is no reliable way to distinguish a woman experiencing complications from an illegal abortion from a woman who has suffered a miscarriage.

Because doctors cannot distinguish a spontaneous miscarriage from an abortion, the government will lack the evidence necessary to support a conviction against women who have early abortions.

Salvadoran lawyer Dennis Munoz, who has defended more women convicted of abortion-related offenses than any other lawyer in the country, explained it this way:

> Yes, there are many illegal abortions in El Salvador for sure. But how do you prosecute them without evidence? There's a rule here called *corpus delecti*, which requires the state to prove a crime has taken place.[24] It's much easier to prove the crime if you have a body. To catch an early abortion, you need evidence that it's provoked. Undissolved pills in the vagina or a perforated uterus. There has to be some evidence.

Munoz's observation helps explain why the law has generated a line of prosecutions against women who lost their pregnancies at or close to full term, rather than prosecute cases against women who took drugs or hired someone to terminate an unwanted pregnancy. What Munoz's observation does not explain is why reports to police are generated almost exclusively from public hospitals. When El Salvador sought to enlist doctors in enforcing its abortion ban, only those working in public hospitals complied.

The Cases: Public Hospitals, Poor Women, and Police Reports

My hunch was that a doctor's willingness to report a woman for suspected abortion would reflect his or her personal beliefs about abortion. It turns out that I was wrong.

The first comprehensive investigation in El Salvador traced the origins of abortion prosecutions over the ten-year time frame from 2001 to 2011. By traveling across the country and visiting every criminal court, researchers identified 129 abortion prosecutions.[25] A doctor's report triggered the great majority of these prosecutions. Yet not a single one of these reports was made by a doctor in private practice, seeing a paying patient.[26]

I wondered what might make a doctor at a public hospital more willing to act on suspicions, so I decided to try talking to a doctor who had made a report. This task was complicated because the doctors' police reports are anonymous. In the end, I settled for interviews with two doctors: one whom I knew believed doctors should not report their patients, and the other whom I suspected of having reported a patient.

Interview with Dr. Rosario

Dr. Bernadette Rosario (pseudonym) was born into a medical family and raised in San Salvador. In her mid-forties, Rosario is a powerful woman who has served in the country's Ministry of Health, as well as on the faculty of the country's foremost medical school. Her office is in Colonia Médica, home to the country's leading private medical practices. The neighborhood is only a mile or two from the public hospital where Beatriz waited out her ordeal. But whereas the entry to the public hospital was crowded with street vendors, ragged children, and dilapidated cars, Colonia Médica is tranquil. It consists of several tall buildings arrayed around a circular patch of grass. In the middle of the grass, a bronze statue of an enormous golden hand cradles a tiny baby in its palm.

"Can you tell me about doctor-patient confidentiality rights in El Salvador?" I asked at the start of our conversation.[27]

I needn't have worried about putting her on the defensive. Rosario looked me straight in the eye and answered, "Here, the right to confidentiality comes with a price tag. Patients at the private hospitals buy their privacy—no one ever reveals their secrets. You could lose your medical license and spend three to six years in prison for breaching patient confidentiality. And besides, they're your patients—you know them, or their families, or their friends. Your reputation and your livelihood depend on them."

"What percentage of Salvadorans go to private doctors and hospitals?" I asked.

"Three percent. Maybe five percent." She smiled and shook her head when she saw the look on my face.

I found it hard to believe that all the elevator buildings in the Colonia Médica, the medical offices, and the small specialty hospitals served only three hundred thousand of the country's six million residents.[28]

Rosario continued, "Eighty percent of Salvadorans get their care from public hospitals located throughout the country. The rest, mostly those who are retired or on pensions, get something in between."

I'm not naive about the difference between the quality of health care received by rich and poor Americans. Generally speaking, we too live in a tiered health-care system.[29] Still, I wondered how poor women lost their right to confidentiality simply because they couldn't afford to see a private doctor.

"Why aren't doctors in public hospitals worried about breaching patient confidentiality when they report women for abortion?" I asked.

Rosario answered, "Well, a lot of doctors think they're obligated to report women they suspect of having done something to terminate their pregnancies; they do it because they think the law says they must. And then there are those who report because they really believe it's a terrible crime to terminate a pregnancy and they want to see the law enforced. And, of course, doctors in public hospitals typically are young, hoping to build a reputation and then to start a private practice. They'll do what they need to do to avoid conflict with their nurses or their superiors."

"Do women know the public hospital doctors might report them?" I asked.

"It depends," said Rosario. "Some of them are savvy enough to know exactly what sort of things separate the public from the private hospitals. But my guess is that most women don't know. No one talks much about abortion or the law, and even if they knew, poor women seek care at public hospitals simply because they're bleeding to death and they have no other option."

Rosario had done little to conceal her opinion that patient confidentiality should preclude abortion reports to police. But then, she was allied with the opponents of the abortion law. I'd gotten her name from the activists working to overturn the ban. I wondered if health-care providers who supported the ban, who believed abortion was murder, nonetheless felt bound by patient confidentiality.

Dr. Diaz's Interview

There is a stigma to breaking the Hippocratic oath, which is at the heart of how doctors understand their ethical obligations to their patients. So I knew it would be difficult to find a doctor willing to speak openly about breaching patient confidentiality. Moreover, because abortion indictments and prosecutions are unpublished, I lacked easy access to the names of doctors who served as witnesses in these cases. I caught a break here, although I didn't know why until later.

In 2002, Dr. Marvin Diaz (pseudonym) was a young attending physician working in the emergency room of a public hospital while training as an obstetrician.[30] There, he treated a woman named Karina Climaco, whose mother had brought her in; she was hemorrhaging and passing blood clots. Diaz examined Karina and found evidence of both uterine enlargement and placental tissue in her vaginal cavity. According to Karina, after the examination, Diaz called the police. Within hours of her admission to the hospital, police arrived at Karina's mother's apartment, searched her home, and found the cold body of a newborn baby.[31]

Karina was later convicted and imprisoned before being exonerated when her defense lawyers proved she had a spontaneous miscarriage. The case received considerable publicity, and I was able to review the transcript, where I found Diaz's name.

After a number of false starts, I found Diaz's contact information. At first, he insisted I had the wrong person; his surname is common in El Salvador. I persisted, though, and after some back-and-forth, he agreed to meet with me. I didn't understand why until I got to his office.[32] There was a Jewish candelabrum on his otherwise empty desk.

Surprised, I asked, "What's this for?" There are no more than a hundred Jews living in El Salvador.[33] Diaz responded that he was a Converso, descended from a long line of Jews who ostensibly converted to

Catholicism during the Spanish inquisition of 1492, and who survived by hiding their religious identity and practices.[34] He said he'd guessed I was Jewish from my name. He had guessed correctly, although I'd never considered my surname, invented at Ellis Island two generations ago, to be particularly Jewish.

"That's why I agreed to meet you," he told me. We chatted a little in broken Hebrew and, oddly moved, I turned to the conversation at hand.

Diaz remembered the sequence of events around the reporting differently than Karina had: "It was her mother who found out about the baby when she noticed blood underneath the bed, and it was the mother who pressed charges. In any case, all we did was come and perform some tests to figure out if the woman had been pregnant. It didn't mean we were going to call the police, but somehow the police got there at that moment."[35]

"Would you have reported her, though?" I asked.

"No," he answered, "we are supposed to protect what our patients tell us and we do."

"Even though the law says that you have to report it?" I asked.

"Yes," he answered. "And I have to be sincere with what I am about to say. In El Salvador, the law is not applied to everyone, but rather only to certain individuals. For example, in private hospitals, things are done where no one really knows what happened except for the doctor and the patient."

Diaz is now in private practice; his office is in the same neighborhood as Rosario's. I wanted to probe Diaz's comfort level with the outright ban on abortion.

"How does it feel as a doctor to see a ten-year-old girl, pregnant as the result of incest?" I asked.

"The law here is very strict," he replied. "It says that you can never terminate a pregnancy. There is never an extenuating circumstance. . . . In my medical view, I'd say it was worth it to allow her to have that baby. I've seen people for whom it was hard during the pregnancy because of situations like those, but when the baby is born, the woman's life is completely transformed. I've seen women who come to me and, well, yes, they do need support, and that's what they don't have here. You can have a difficult situation, but as long as you're supported, you will continue to go forward. You'll be able to overcome any obstacle."

My conversation with Diaz shook me at many levels. It was oddly refreshing to meet someone who supported the abortion law. He was not troubled by the law's failure to make exceptions in "hard" cases like incest, which after all have nothing to do with the fetus's moral status. Instead, he was bothered by the hypocrisy that permits wealthy women to evade the law.

Diaz saw abortion as murder.

Yet, even though he supported the abortion ban, Diaz was unwilling to acknowledge that he'd ever divulged patient confidences, even in the past. He did not want credit for having alerted the police about Karina's dead baby. Instead, he gave me a flimsy story about how it might have been her mother who called the police.

What bears noting is that both Diaz and Rosario portrayed medical confidentiality as a commodity. Rich women buy their privacy from private doctors. Poor women arrive at the country's public hospitals too broke to go anywhere else. They lack the funds to ensure their secrets will be kept private.

The story of how abortion is prosecuted in El Salvador begins with this reality: doctors at public hospitals call the police and poor women are prosecuted.

POOR, INNOCENT WOMEN
ACCUSED OF ABORTION CRIMES

It helps to remember Diaz's patient, Karina, as we move from the subject of detecting abortion to considering the third consequence of banning abortion in El Salvador: innocent women were prosecuted and convicted of abortion-related crimes.

Karina was reported to police on suspicion of illegal abortion after Diaz treated her in the emergency room of the public hospital. She was hemorrhaging, and the size of her uterus plus the presence of a placenta (also referred to as the afterbirth) left no doubt that she had been pregnant. Where was the baby?

Cases like hers make up over 50 percent of the cases brought against women for abortion.

The Typical Abortion Prosecution in El Salvador

At first, it's hard to see why the crime of abortion would generate cases like Karina's, which involve a dead full-term fetus. The answer lies in what we already know. First, it is hard to detect early abortion. Second, when there is physical evidence that a woman has recently delivered a baby, doctors naturally may suspect foul play. Because there is evidence to support their suspicions, they are more willing to notify the police.

The comprehensive study of all abortion-related prosecutions in the decade between 2001 and 2011 found 129 cases in which women were investigated for abortion-related offenses.[36] That is a lot, if one pictures each prosecution in all its complicated, intimate messiness. But honestly, I was surprised to find that even in a country unequivocally committed to enforcing criminal laws against abortion, there were seldom more than ten or twelve prosecutions a year.

More puzzling still was the fact that close to half of these investigations ultimately did not involve the crime of abortion at all. Instead, these investigations and arrests involved fetuses at or beyond seven months' gestation at the time of their deaths.[37] These are hardly the sort of cases that come to mind when one thinks about making abortion a crime.

These late-term cases wind up playing a larger and larger role as abortion investigations work their way through the Salvadoran criminal justice system. Not all abortion investigations turn into cases that get prosecuted, of course. More often than not, prosecutors opt not to pursue criminal charges. Some cases do move forward, though, and at this point, we see the most startling pattern emerging in the abortion prosecutions: they aren't about abortion at all.

Of the forty-nine Salvadoran women arrested for abortion, only thirteen ultimately were convicted of that crime. Salvadoran law distinguishes between abortion and homicide, treating as homicide any case involving a fetus beyond seven months' gestation. Thus, if it turns out the fetus was beyond seven months' gestation, the charges against the woman are elevated from abortion, which is punishable by two to eight years imprisonment, to homicide, which carries a maximum sentence of fifty years in prison. Of the forty-nine women originally charged with abortion, thirty-six were convicted of aggravated homicide.

The typical abortion prosecution in El Salvador doesn't look at all like what I'd expected. Rather than involving women who obtained early, illegal abortions through the black market, the cases involve women accused of deliberately killing their newborns after delivering them at home.

These cases evoke a visceral revulsion with which I am familiar. The facts behind these prosecutions aren't all that different from some of the cases in the United States involving mothers who kill their children. Here, too, the cases involved mothers who denied or concealed their pregnancies, unattended births, or babies who died after being delivered in toilets. Here, too, the mothers were charged with homicide.

But in these cases in El Salvador, the only crime the mothers seem to have committed is being desperately poor and pregnant, and losing a baby after delivering it at home.

I'll confess that I did not feel much sympathy for these women at first. Perhaps their doctors violated confidentiality, but surely the possibility that a woman has killed her newborn merits a police investigation at the least.

Munoz, the Salvadoran defense lawyer, persuaded me I was wrong.[38] In case after case, the Salvadoran criminal justice system has wrongly convicted poor women of homicide when the only evidence against them was that they had a late miscarriage.

To help me understand the connection between abortion laws and the criminalization of miscarriage, in March 2012 Munoz took me to meet Christina, a former client.

From the Hospital to the Prison: Christina's Story

We visited Christina at her grandmother's home in El Transito, a village two hours outside San Salvador. She began her story at the point when she was seventeen and expecting her second child. Several months into her pregnancy, she and her three-year-old son left El Transito and moved to San Salvador, living in the second bedroom of her mother and stepfather's apartment so that Christina would be close to the public hospital when her baby came.

It was Saturday, October 23, 2004. Earlier that week, Christina and her mother had shopped for new linens and baby clothes, having decided to spend money on the baby rather than on a baby shower. As her mother prepared to leave for work, Christina mentioned that she'd had diarrhea earlier that morning. Neither she nor her mother was alarmed, though. Christina had had stomach problems regularly since her appendix burst, about a year before, and her baby wasn't due for another month or so.

After dinner, when her mother returned from her shift at the tortilla factory, Christina mentioned that her stomach was upset. She lay down on the bed she shared with her three-year-old son. She felt sick, but it didn't feel as if she was having contractions; she knew because she remembered how they'd felt.

Several hours later, she got out of bed and told her mother she couldn't sleep. Her mother made her some tea with sugar.

In the middle of the night, Christina awakened with an urge to go to the bathroom. She sat up in bed and felt a sudden, tremendous pain. The apartment was small, so she managed to get to the bathroom by dragging herself, one hand on each wall. The pain was so intense that she felt she was suffocating. The last thing she remembers is struggling to push open the metal bathroom door.

She woke up in a hospital bed where a woman stood over her demanding, "*Y el bebé?*" ("And the baby?"). As she emerged from the fog of anesthesia, three guards stood at her bedside, asking, "What's your name? Where do you live? How many months pregnant were you?" She kept falling asleep, and they kept shaking her awake, saying, "You have to answer us."

Over the course of long hours of interrogation, she learned that her baby had died. After getting a call from the doctors, police had searched Christina's mother's apartment and found the body in the mess of blood and towels left behind when her mother dragged Christina to the neighbor's waiting truck so they could drive her to the hospital.

Christina had experienced what doctors call "precipitous labor and delivery," in which there is a sudden onset and rapid progression of the birth process.[39] Doctors don't always know why this happens, but one expert on the subject, Dr. Anne Drapkin Lyerly, a professor and obstetrician at the University of North Carolina, offered several explanations for what might have caused Christina's miscarriage.

"My first guess," she said, "involves infection. The fact that she had ongoing gastrointestinal problems is a common sign of infection. In pregnant women, such infections can spread to the amniotic sac, leading to precipitous delivery and/or miscarriage."[40]

Lyerly noted that a quick pathology investigation of the placenta would have revealed the presence or absence of infection. In Christina's case, no such examination was performed. It's not clear whether the government would have paid the costs for such testing, given Christina's impoverished status and her reliance on a public defender. It's not even clear that doctors or prosecutors bothered to preserve her placenta as forensic evidence. The issue is moot, though, as Christina's lawyer never made the request.

Instead, after two or three days at the hospital, Christina was arrested on suspicion of abortion and was transferred, handcuffed and still bleeding, to the police station just outside the women's prison in the city of Ilopango. After a week of interrogations and after the coroner determined that the fetus was beyond seven months' gestation, Christina was charged with homicide.

At her preliminary hearing, the prosecutor argued that Christina must have known she was in labor because she had already had a child. Once a woman experiences labor pains, he claimed, she cannot mistake them for any other sort of pain. Christina killed her child, the state alleged, by not telling someone she was in labor.

The presiding judge told the prosecutor to respect Christina's loss. He dismissed the case for lack of proof.

Fifteen days later, the prosecution claimed it had "new evidence," although Christina's defense team never learned what it was, and Christina's case was reopened. She was assigned a new public defender, whom she didn't meet until the day of her preliminary hearing. Once again, the state had charged her with *homocidio culposo*—our version of manslaughter. The crime carried a potential sentence of two to eight years. This time, the judge let the case go to trial.

At trial, her new lawyer failed to object when the judges decided to convict Christina of a far more serious crime than the one with which she had been charged: *homicidio agravado*, or aggravated homicide. The judges justified this heightened penalty by referencing the innocence of the victim, and by once more invoking the notion that, as an experienced mother, Christina must have known she was in labor.

Christina was convicted on the theory that, by failing to get medical help, she caused her baby's death. Aggravated homicide (*homicidio agravado*) carries a much higher penalty than manslaughter (*homicidio culposo*), and Christina was sentenced to thirty years.

I asked Lyerly what she thought of the state's claim that Christina must have known she was in labor.

"There's no logic to the court's position," she said.

> There was no reason why she should have known it was labor, and a lot of reasons why she shouldn't have—her history of gastrointestinal trouble actually means she was unlikely to know it was different; women deliver precipitously all the time; vaginal birth changes the musculature such that later deliveries tend to be much faster than first-time births. And given that she was a month away from her due date, she was more likely to think she was not in labor.[41]

Inside Ilopango, the women's prison, Christina met eight or nine women convicted of abortion-related crimes. Amid the hundreds of women imprisoned in the crowded women's cells of Ilopango, they stuck together.

Like all prisons, Ilopango had a social hierarchy. According to Christina, the drug traffickers and mass-murderers were treated the best. The other inmates applauded them. The worst treatment, by contrast, was reserved for those who had killed their children. "*Te comiste a tus hijos*" ("You ate your children"), they called out in passing to her and to the others incarcerated for abortion-related offenses.

After almost two years in prison, one of the other abortion inmates introduced Christina to Munoz, who was her lawyer. Munoz quickly spotted the judicial error in Christina's case. In El Salvador, as in the United States, judges are not permitted to revise the charges against a criminal defendant. Only the prosecutor can determine what crimes to charge.

Munoz submitted a motion seeking a new trial, arguing the court had overstepped its bounds by convicting her of a crime with which she had not been charged. The state quickly responded, offering to release Christina for time served. Christina was happy to go home to her son and her family, and opted not to seek a new trial and the chance to clear her name.

For Munoz, Christina's case was just one among a score of similar cases, one in which justice came relatively easily.

Late Miscarriages, Wrongful Convictions, and Implications for the Abortion Ban

In El Salvador, the battle over the abortion ban increasingly focuses on cases like Christina's. The problem of wrongful convictions in such cases emerged as a surprise finding of the 2009 conference between Nicaragua and El Salvador, convened by opponents of the abortion bans in both countries. Few in attendance anticipated that they would work on cases of women who never wanted to terminate their pregnancies in the first place. Yet the stories told by defense lawyers like Munoz made it clear that, in El Salvador, cases like Christina's had become commonplace.

To be sure, before the 1998 ban, women were convicted of homicide in cases involving dead newborns. But those cases did not originate in calls to police from public hospitals involving women who had had late-term miscarriages. Instead, they involved babies whose bodies, when found, showed signs of having been born alive.

At first, abortion-rights activists struggled over whether to work on this type of case, rather than strategizing ways to overturn the ban. After all, they had joined together with a specific goal: persuading the government to make exceptions to the ban. The activists call themselves the Agrupación Ciudadana por la Despenalización del Aborto Terapéu-tico Ético y Eugenésico (Citizens Group for the Decriminalization of Ethical, Eugenic and Theraputic Abortion), or the Agrupación Ciudad-ana, for short. Their wordy name reflects their goal of reinstating the abortion law that governed the country prior to 1998: a ban with the exceptions for cases involving rape, incest, fetal anomaly, or threats to maternal life or health. The group comprises lawyers, academics, stu-dents, and activists, who write grants to fund their work, which origi-nally consisted of social media publicity and street-level activism, such as parades and protests.[42]

As I learned from one of the group's founders, Morena Herrera, many felt disturbed by cases like Christina's and worried they were a distraction from the battle over the abortion law.[43]

Eventually, though, the Agrupación Ciudadana dedicated itself to defending these women and to protesting the pattern of wrongful con-victions.[44] Its lawyers undertook an investigation of the cases of all the women incarcerated on abortion-related offenses.

On April 1, 2014, the Agrupación Ciudadana submitted seventeen petitions to the legislative assembly, each of which demanded a legal pardon for a woman serving a sentence for an abortion-related homi-cide. The seventeen cases included every Salvadoran woman then incar-cerated for abortion-related homicide.[45]

According to Munoz and his colleagues, there was *not a single guilty woman* among those who had been imprisoned for these crimes since 1998. It is a stunning claim. Yet the facts behind their cases are so similar as to be interchangeable. If it could happen to one woman, why not seventeen?

Each of the seventeen women was serving a sentence of between thirty to forty years. The majority were poor, uneducated, and young; over a quarter were illiterate and over half had not made it past third grade.[46] All had experienced obstetrical complications at some point during their pregnancies, resulting in late miscarriages. They gave birth unattended. Their newborns were stillborn or died shortly after birth. The women bled so heavily that they sought care at a hospital, where they were arrested.

The Campaign for the 17, as it is known in El Salvador, has had surprising success. On January 22, 2015, the legislative assembly announced its decision to pardon Guadalupe, one of the seventeen women.[47] It was one of the only pardons issued by the government in years, owing in part to the fact that in order to pardon a crime, the state must acknowledge its own error.

Scarcely a month later, the Agrupación Ciudadana secured another victory, this time for a woman who had been incarcerated after her doctor reported her to police for a suspected abortion. She had been sentenced to thirty years in prison for having brought about the death of her five-month-old fetus. In April 2015, after she had served fifteen months in prison, the judge found that her doctor had violated the obligation to maintain patient confidentiality and, in addition, that the prosecution had failed to prove that the baby had been born alive.[48] In May 2016, a third woman—Maria Teresa Rivera—was released after serving four years of a forty-year sentence, when the state acknowledged lack of evidence of live birth or criminal intent.[49]

These cases are travesties. It is almost too painful to imagine what it feels like to go into labor suddenly, alone, far from the hospital. To be carried to the hospital, hemorrhaging and in pain, having lost the pregnancy. To arrive there only to be accused of killing your baby, by a state that never had evidence the baby was born alive, let alone that you intentionally killed it.

It is hard for a legal system to admit that it got things wrong. So these exonerations are a tribute to the Salvadoran legal system, as well as to the Agrupación lawyers. Yet these victories remain exceptions.

The 2014 legislative assembly rejected the pardons of the remaining fourteen women, in some cases without comment, in other cases giving explanations such as "risk of recidivism due to poor social status and lack of education."[50]

The Agrupación Ciudadana continues to fight, but it seems that for every woman whose freedom it has secured, there are several more women newly convicted. By 2015, Las 17 had become twenty-four, which was the grand total of the original seventeen, minus three, for the women exonerated, and plus eight for the newcomers. Munoz and the other Agrupación lawyers know all the newly convicted women. The facts of their cases are familiar by now. But the work of overturning their convictions proceeds slowly, case by case.

ASSESSING THE CONSEQUENCES OF BANNING ABORTION

What are we to make of what has happened in El Salvador under the abortion ban? The effort to assess the law's consequences feels like a charged, partisan endeavor. At the end of the day, it seems that abortion exists in a world in which, as Friedrich Nietzsche observed, "There are no facts, only interpretations."[51]

I can't tell you how to interpret the story I've told you. But I can assure you that it would be largely the same story, any place around the globe.

Abortion Will Still Happen

No one ever claimed that banning abortion would eliminate it. What's surprising is that there is no evidence that banning abortion reduces the abortion rate. It is possible, of course, that the ban makes a difference at the individual level, leading some women to keep their unwanted pregnancies, rather than having abortions.

But we know that there can't be millions or even thousands of such women, because if there were, then we would see higher birth rates in countries with abortion bans than we do in similar countries with more permissive laws. We don't. El Salvador's birth rates are no higher now than they were before the ban, in 1998. Nor are they significantly different from those of their neighbors with more permissive abortion laws: Honduras, Costa Rica, and Panama.

Banning Abortion Has an Impact on Women and Girls

When abortion is illegal, it is unsafe. In El Salvador, scores of women die every year from illegal abortions.[52] They aren't the daughters of the elite, whose money helps them find safe, private ways to end their unwanted pregnancies. They are the women who live far from cities, in cinder-block homes with dirt floors and no running water. They are the women who continue to use coat hangers in the age of the Internet because they cannot afford to purchase abortion drugs online.

In addition, banning abortion changes the lives of girls, who, because they cannot get an abortion, become mothers as teenagers. El Salvador has one of the highest rates of unwed teen motherhood in the world; a Pan American Health Organization report noted that one in four births in El Salvador is to women ages fifteen to nineteen.[53]

In El Salvador, having a child at age fourteen isn't simply a cause for shame in the eyes of a religious community. It also increases the odds of a life lived in crushing poverty, of marginal education and employment, of vulnerability to the violence and chaos that scores the lives of the poorest Salvadorans.

Some girls, faced with that prospect, opt to kill themselves. Government statistics reveal that three out of eight maternal deaths in El Salvador are the result of suicide among pregnant girls under nineteen.[54] Many of these girls have suffered rape and sexual abuse, and are silenced by the shame of these humiliations, in addition to the stigma of pregnancy.

Across the globe, one finds similar trends. Where abortion is illegal, there are high rates of medical complications and deaths due to illegal abortion. There are high rates of teen pregnancies. Pregnant teens commit suicide.

For opponents of the abortion ban, each of these trends is a clear indictment of the law.

For the ban's supporters, though, I imagine these indirect consequences on the lives of women and girls are viewed as part of a picture that includes other lives—those that begin at conception and that the law must therefore acknowledge and protect.

The Law Won't Catch the Women It Targets

The most intense condemnation of abortion typically is reserved for women whose motives seem entirely selfish. The wealthy, married woman for whom a baby is inconvenient or the woman who has an abortion because she wants to be able to wear her bikini. The women whom Mayora, an outspoken supporter of El Salvador's ban, decried as "wanting an abortion for any reason, or for no reason at all."[55]

What we learn from El Salvador is that the law can't catch such women. Illegal abortion no longer has to involve "abortion doctors." Ready access to abortion drugs and the fact that abortion is almost always indistinguishable from miscarriage mean most privileged women who have early abortions will escape detection, even when things go wrong and they wind up in the hospital.

What is true for El Salvador will be doubly true in wealthier countries, where women will have many more options for ending an unwanted pregnancy in a relatively safe, discrete way.

The Law Will Catch Innocent Women

The law will catch women who arouse their doctor's suspicion. In El Salvador, the women accused of abortion are among the poorest women in the country. They seldom know the doctors they meet at the public hospitals where they get care. And in most cases, their doctors understand very little about them. Their doctors don't know anyone who lives as these women do—with outhouses, dirt floors, no running water. These women are so poor and marginal that their doctors find it hard to understand their responses to crisis. Their world is so unfamiliar that it becomes possible for doctors, and later prosecutors and judges, to project their own fears onto it, inventing motives for crimes in the process.

To the woman in labor who fell down the steep path to the latrine, they impute the intention to conceal her delivery and kill her child. She must have wanted the child to suffocate in the muck so that she could avoid the burden of raising it on her own, with no husband and no money.[56]

The lucky ones have lawyers who spend years undoing the errors that led to their convictions. But there is no way to undo the harm brought on by a state that took a woman in crisis, having arrived at a hospital hemorrhaging and in pain, having given birth alone, having lost a child, and treated her like a criminal.

It is tempting to say these cases will not arise in the United States. Surely, our defense lawyers would protect the rights of the wrongly accused, insisting that the state prove the woman's guilt rather than being able to presume it.

But here, too, doctors can be suspicious of women who live on the margins of society, of those they meet only in the emergency rooms of public hospitals.[57] The consequences of making abortion a crime include a pattern we've already seen, in the context of prosecutions of women for ingesting illicit drugs during pregnancy. As I discuss in detail in chapter 5, these prosecutions have disproportionately targeted poor, black women, many of whom were seeking prenatal care at public hospitals. Ban abortion and that pattern will intensify. The hospital will increasingly become the site of a crime scene investigation, and poor women will be the suspects.

CONCLUSION

We saw in the first chapter how abortion opponents look to the law to reinforce their moral vision. In this chapter, we see the pragmatic limitations of the law.

The conceit of the law is that the moral stance and the practical consequences will move in one direction. Can we honestly say this is true about the abortion ban?

At best, the results are ambiguous. It is a law whose only tangible benefit beyond its moral message is hypothetical: there must be some women whom the law deters, even if there aren't enough to cause a rise in birth rates.

Are these hypothetical lives saved enough to offset the consequences we've seen in El Salvador?

I can't make that calculus for you, but make no mistake: these consequences will follow us as we turn to the question of restricting abortions in the United States.

We'll be tempted to ignore them, because they play no part in our pitched battle over abortion law. But if we keep them in mind, they'll permit us to see the shallow and misleading nature of our abortion war.

THREE

THE REDDEST STATE: OKLAHOMA'S LONG BATTLE OVER ABORTION LAW

The best place to watch the US battle over abortion law play out is in a state where a strong majority identifies as pro-life, and lawmakers are determined to pass laws opposing abortion. I wanted to understand the way abortion opponents viewed the law. Did they look to the law for moral condemnation, as I'd seen abortion opponents do in El Salvador? How might things change, in their eyes, were abortion to be banned?

I couldn't hope to learn how the pro-life movement viewed abortion laws without leaving my home, in the blue state of California. And so, in 2013, I went to Oklahoma.

As most Oklahomans will proudly tell you, it is a really, really red state. After Democrats lost every single county in the state in the 2008 and 2012 presidential elections, Oklahomans laid claim to being "the reddest state in the country."[1] In 2016, Republican Donald Trump won over 65 percent of the vote. His Democratic opponent Hillary Clinton earned less than 30 percent.

Oklahoma caught my eye when I first began thinking about visiting a red state because of the pace at which Oklahoma passed its pro-life legislation. In less than a decade, it brought its abortion laws right to the limits of what was permissible under federal law as dictated by the US Supreme Court. This fervor has earned Oklahoma top ratings in the Americans United for Life's annual legislative report card for over a decade.[2]

Oklahoma also has the virtue of being home to several law schools, which meant I had a place to begin seeking contacts. The Oklahoma City University Law School, located blocks from the capitol, has alumni serving throughout state government. I reached out to former dean Lawrence Hellman, who, along with Professors Arthur LeFrancois and Andrew Spiropoulos, introduced me to lawmakers, lobbyists, doctors, and activists at the forefront of the state's battles over abortion law.

I rented a house in a modest neighborhood in Oklahoma City and moved in for the hot summer months of 2013. And I started listening.

WHEN OKLAHOMA WAS A DEMOCRATIC STATE

In 1973, Oklahoma was a solidly Democratic state. Not only did the people vote Democratic in national elections, Democrats held both chambers and the governor's office. The largest religious organization in the state, the Southern Baptist Convention, supported legalized abortion.[3]

Anyone hoping to understand abortion politics in Oklahoma must sooner or later reckon with the impact and the legacies of two men: Tony Lauinger and Bernest Cain. Since 1973, Lauinger has devoted himself singularly to the cause of ending legalized abortion. He's never held office, yet even the legislators I met spoke of the bills Lauinger introduced, the laws he got passed, and the thickly powerful pro-life coalition he commands.

From 1978 to 2006, Lauinger's nemesis was state senator Bernest Cain. In his capacity as chair of the Senate Human Resources Committee, working at the behest of the Senate president pro tempore, Cain spent close to thirty years preventing antiabortion bills from reaching the Senate floor. His district was the most liberal in the state, which insulated him from the increasingly socially conservative statewide electorate. By keeping pro-life bills stalled in his committee, he single-handedly kept Oklahoma from passing laws that restricted access to abortion.

By the end of his time in office, Cain was playing a frenzied game of whack-a-mole. Both state houses were filled with legislators elected on promises to end legalized abortion. The backlog of antiabortion bills was legion. Districts had swung so far to the right that his fellow Democrats no longer thanked him for protecting them from the political fallout they would have faced, had they been forced to cast a vote their constituents might have viewed as "pro-abortion." Whether for reasons of moral conviction or political expedience, most Democrats and Republicans wanted to pass laws restricting abortion.

But our story begins decades before then, back in the days when abortion had just become legal.

Building a Pro-Life Movement in Oklahoma: 1973–2004

Lauinger was alone when, in 1973, he began fighting against legalized abortion. He was a Catholic in a state where 60 percent of the population was Southern Baptist and only 4 percent was Catholic.

In an article in the National Right to Life Committee (NRLC)'s *World Magazine*, Lauinger's entry into antiabortion activism is described: "In 1972, he was preparing to become a father for the first time. He reveled in being able to feel his baby kicking inside his wife's womb. When the Supreme Court legalized abortion, several months after his daughter's birth, he felt like he'd been hit in the face by a four by four."[4]

Born into exceptional wealth, Lauinger was thirty in 1972, when he felt called into service in response to *Roe v. Wade*.[5] He began by founding Tulsans for Life, an affiliate of the NRLC. By 1978, he was president of Oklahomans for Life and a member of the NRLC's board of directors.

It is hard to remember a time when the battle over abortion was not at the center of our public discourse. Kristen Luker's 1984 book, *Abortion and the Politics of Motherhood*, is a masterful history of antiabortion activism in the years immediately following *Roe*.[6] Her book helps set the context for understanding Lauinger's work.

Luker's research on pro-life activism in the years following the Supreme Court's *Roe* ruling documents a movement built largely by individuals who were shocked by the court's decision. They had interpreted the relative silence about abortion as a collective agreement that the fetus was a person, and that abortion ends the life of a child.[7] United by their shared opposition to abortion on moral grounds, yet lacking political experience or community-organizing backgrounds, early pro-life activists gained a foothold in faith-based communities.

In the context of religious communities, Lauinger forged an alliance that is central to the power of Oklahoma's pro-life movement. By the early 1980s, Lauinger was working to mobilize Oklahoma's largest faith-based organization to join him in fighting against legalized abortion.

In order to explain the way pro-life politics evolved in Oklahoma, I have to say a bit about the centrality of organized religion in public life. God is ubiquitous in Oklahoma. That's silly, of course, because for those who believe in God, by definition, God is everywhere. But in Oklahoma, unlike California, God is really out in public. God surfaces not only in clichéd billboards and bumper stickers but also in casual conversations.

I feel pretty grounded in my faith as a Jew. I'm not put off when others make reference to God when describing their lives, the decisions they've made, or the way they've coped with adversity. There was something foreign to me, though, about the way so many Oklahomans spoke of a personal relationship with God and of the need to live, and to pass abortion laws, in accordance with God's dictates.

To the extent that I was going to understand what folks meant when they invoked God in our conversations about abortion and the law, I knew I needed to understand more about the Southern Baptist Convention. There are many different types of evangelical communities in Oklahoma, and I don't mean to suggest that the Southern Baptists speak for all of them. It's just that the Southern Baptists are by far the largest: 60 percent of Oklahomans identify as Southern Baptists.

So, on a hot July morning in 2013, I traveled to the state headquarters of the Southern Baptist Convention to meet with Dr. Anthony

Jordan, its executive director. The five-story office building on Oklahoma City's north side houses an organization that represents over 1,830 churches in Oklahoma. It publishes a paper with the third-largest circulation in the state, a weekly called the *Baptist Messenger*.[8] In a sense, one might see Jordan as the voice of the state's majority.

Jordan's involvement with abortion politics didn't begin until 1985. That year, he was asked to preach at a statewide conference for Baptist pastors. He was invited to speak about any moral issue. Because he and his wife had struggled with infertility, he had a personal connection to the issue of adoption, and to the way in which legalized abortion reduced the number of babies put up for adoption. He decided to preach about abortion.

He began by listing his reasons for opposing abortion, which included both medical and biblical sources. But the speech took a personal turn when he mentioned a recent news story about the discovery of sixteen thousand body parts found behind an abortion clinic in California. "At that point," he said, "I asked my wife to bring up our five-month-old adopted daughter. 'When I read about the trash heap,' I told the crowd, 'it bothered me even more so because this little girl. . . . If it hadn't been for the Baptist Children's Home opening their doors to her Catholic mother, she could have been in a trash heap.'

"The entire room, including me, was in tears," he said. His eyes were wet even now, remembering the moment.

In the wake of that speech, Jordan and the Southern Baptist Convention joined forces with Lauinger and the Oklahoma Right to Life organization. Together, they developed a series of projects and initiatives. Foremost among the public demonstrations is the annual Rose Day rally, which began in the mid-1970s when two Catholic women brought roses to their state legislators to mark the anniversary of *Roe v. Wade*. This small gesture evolved into a yearly event that by 2016 saw an estimated twenty thousand Oklahomans converge on the state capitol, each bearing roses for their lawmakers. Today, Oklahoma's Rose Day is one of the nation's largest annual pro-life gatherings.[9] In the early years, pro-life legislators invited the activists into the state house, letting them sit on the floor during their rally. In recent years, the crowd has been so big it fills the Senate floor and both legislative galleries. The rally features speakers ranging from the governor to national pro-life leaders. Roses are everywhere.

On a more quotidian level, the church began offering support, along with ministry, through pregnancy resource centers. Jordan's church created Hope Pregnancy Center, one of the first in the state. It is staffed by volunteer community members and funded by donations and by the state of Oklahoma, through its sponsored "Choose Life" license plate program. The center, along with several hundred similar centers around the state, offers pregnancy tests, ultrasounds, and aid to women facing unplanned pregnancies. Jordan explained the mission of these centers, "We offer to stand beside the woman, supporting her through parenting training, placement of her baby with adopted family, if they wish. We support her either way."

The Southern Baptist Convention's work is not limited to rallies and counseling. Indeed, its most significant impact may be the mobilization of a powerful voting bloc. Under Jordan's leadership, the Southern Baptist Convention publishes election brochures that list candidates' positions on abortion. Jordan told me that he couldn't vote for a pro-choice candidate today, and his voting guides help similar-minded voters follow suit.

With at least nine hundred thousand members identifying as Southern Baptists, Jordan confidently noted, "We're organized and we can move." They've developed an alert system, dividing the state into districts to get out the vote. With a phone call, his office can mobilize forty-two separate organizations.

Until 2004, all that mobilization had little effect on the statewide abortion laws. "We had the numbers," Jordan noted. "I knew where people stood on the abortion issue in my constituency. I knew the number of churches, the number of Catholics, and the number of nondenominational Christians. But the Capitol wouldn't move."

I knew why. I'd already had lunch with Senator Bernest Cain.

Block That Bill: The Career of Senator Bernest Cain

Over lunch in a crowded restaurant where suited patrons stomped off the March rain and greeted one another with cheery backslaps and clasped handshakes, former state senator Bernest Cain told me about his relationship with God.[10]

"It's always been a religious deal to me," he said. "I knew my work at forestalling abortion bills was only a holding pattern. I never looked at it as a success; I never celebrated my victories. It had to be dealt with spiritually. I've done what I've done because I've worked to be true to my faith as a Unitarian.

"The hypocrisy of wealthy Republicans aggravates me," he said. "I think they've gotten away with making abortion a litmus test, more so than gay rights, because of class and gender. Abortion affects poor women, not men." Having seen firsthand which women were most affected when El Salvador banned abortion, I knew all too well what Cain meant.

What he said about gay rights made sense to me too. It's not that the battle for gay rights was easily won, but think of the speed with which activists were able to secure those rights. In the face of AIDS, in an era in which the president took years to acknowledge that millions of gay men were dying, activists got the Food and Drug Administration to accelerate the drug approval process. Two decades later, they had won rights ranging from freedom from discrimination to the right to marry.

The triumph of gay rights is a reflection, as Cain suggests, of the relative power of privileged gay men compared to poor women of color. Gay men (and women) vote. Political candidates ignore or insult them at their peril. By contrast, the women most affected by abortion policies aren't organized into a voting bloc. Many aren't even old enough to vote. Women's options, when facing an unwanted pregnancy, depend upon their financial resources. We saw it in El Salvador, and we see it here. Those with money have better options than those without. And the poorest women are unlikely to command the ear of a senator.

Cain paid an enormous price for his commitment to protect abortion rights. Although Cain is most proud of work he did on other issues—child support and aid to the elderly poor—he is remembered and reviled for his stance on abortion. By the end of his three decades in office, he feared for his life.

"Some of these people hated me," he said. Six years after leaving office, he still feels the burden of his legacy. "I made a lot of enemies, which limits my ability to serve as a retiree and a volunteer."

Cain never campaigned on a reproductive rights platform. He didn't even think about abortion during his first campaign, back in 1978:

> My opponent was a John Birch–type incumbent who wanted to fire gay teachers. She voted against the Equal Rights Amendment.
>
> I'd left the Baptist church a few years before, after spending a summer in 1972 working as a missionary in Center City, Philadelphia. I was in my third year of Baptist Bible College in Texas. I'd had a hard year because I'd begun to question the notion that the Bible is the word of God. I'd already decided that virgins didn't have babies. And then, in Philly I saw girls from the ghettos, black and Italian young girls. I came home worried that their lives were ruined as a result of having babies so young.
>
> By the end of that year, they kicked me out of Bible College. I finished school at the University of Oklahoma, where I later got a law degree and completed the course work for a PhD in political science. I was working at the university in education, setting standards for county governments. The issues that mattered to me then embarrass me now: mandatory minimum sentences and capital punishment. I favored them both. And I also felt strongly about protecting the civil rights of gay teachers.
>
> The gay community organized around my campaign. I won by 175 votes. There was a big fight over seating me; it was such a close election. After that first race, though, I knew how to organize. I walked door-to-door, precinct by precinct. I held my seat even after the Right to Life turned poor churchgoing whites into Republicans. Even after 1986, when Tony [Lauinger] started mailing my constituents at election time saying I was for killing babies.

OKLAHOMA'S RED SHIFT

Everything about abortion law in Oklahoma began to change between 2004 and 2006, the final two years of Cain's tenure.

As Jordan of the Southern Baptist Convention put it, "In 2004, politics finally began to reflect the true nature of Oklahoma." It was and remains a state in which a large majority of the public identifies as social conservatives.

The Law

In September 1990, Oklahoma voters passed a term-limits law, State Question 632, limiting service in the state legislature to twelve years. The consequences of this amendment to the state constitution weren't felt until 2004, when the first group of lawmakers termed out. Certainly the most obvious change was the rapid shift in political control over the House, first, and then the Senate, from Democratic to Republican hands.

Professor Andrew Spiropoulos explained how it had happened: "Term limits plus the candidacy of Barack Obama turned the state red almost overnight," he said.[11] Spiropoulos knew firsthand how Oklahoma suddenly went "pro-life." In 2005, he took a two-year leave of absence from his job teaching law at Oklahoma City University in order to serve as the Oklahoma State House Policy Advisor. In that capacity, he was in charge of helping the new Speaker of the House determine and implement the Republican agenda.

Abortion was a big part of the Republican agenda because of the central role it played in unifying constituents within the Republican coalition. Spiropoulos said, "Urban Republicans always needed a coalition of rural voters to win here, and these rural voters are pro-life and 'pro-marriage.'" (He clarified that by "pro-marriage," he actually meant anti–gay marriage.) The pro-marriage issue won't sustain the coalition, he conjectured, because more libertarian urban Republicans will defect. Hence, abortion has become the central unifying issue for Oklahoma's Republican Party.

In spring 2006, a bill requiring minors to obtain parental consent became the first antiabortion provision signed into law. It was quickly followed by a bevy of laws, including provisions barring the use of state funds or public facilities to provide abortions, mandating ultrasounds, banning abortion after twenty weeks' gestation, restricting the prescription of RU-486, and prohibiting insurance companies from offering abortion coverage.[12]

Spiropoulos attributed the extraordinary volume of abortion laws passed as a response to Cain's having blocked the laws for so long:

> The most important consequence of Cain's single-handed thwarting of majority sentiment is that he created such an intense blockage in the system and waves of resentment that, when the Republicans took over, it exploded in a flood of new laws. If Cain had not blocked everything, a few of the laws would have passed over the years and, arguably, there wouldn't have been such a rush to pass everything but the kitchen sink—there would have been new pro-life legislation, but the efforts would have been more measured.

Now I understood how Oklahoma had suddenly emerged as a pro-life legislative powerhouse.

None of the laws Oklahoma passed were new. They simply passed every measure enacted by other pro-life states, along with the occasional model bill drafted by Americans United for Life.

The laws cover a broad range of issues. Some of the laws, such as a ban on sex-selective abortion, are plainly symbolic. Women seeking abortions in Oklahoma, as in other states, need not provide a reason for terminating their pregnancies. There is no way to enforce this provision.

Other laws have had a direct impact on the delivery of reproductive health care in the state. For example, one state law forbids the use of public funds or facilities for the provision of abortion services. This law bars doctors at the University of Oklahoma hospital—the state's leading health-care center—from providing abortions for any reasons other than rape, incest, or medical necessity. The ban's most dramatic consequences are seen in cases involving poor women, who learn, typically halfway through their pregnancies, that their fetuses have severe anomalies.

Consider what happens when a poor woman finds out that her fetus has trisomy 18, a condition that causes severe developmental delays due to an extra chromosome 18. As anomalies go, it's fairly common—one in 2,500 pregnancies, and one in 6,000 births. Most of the time, the woman miscarries. For those who survive, life is precarious and profoundly limited. Only 10 percent will reach their first birthday. Those who live require full-time, institutionalized care.[13]

Yet unless this pregnant woman has money to pay for a private abortion—which by mid-trimester, when these anomalies typically are discovered, will cost thousands, rather than hundreds, of dollars—she must continue her pregnancy.

Nor is the impact of these new abortion laws limited to the poorest Oklahomans. Indeed, one of the men I interviewed remarked that the laws already have affected him personally. When he and his wife were expecting their first child, his wife's obstetrician advised them to do their routine twenty-week ultrasound at eighteen weeks, earlier than called for by the national standard of care. Because state law now bans abortions after twenty weeks, the doctor worried that waiting would risk their ability to terminate the pregnancy in the event the tests revealed a serious fetal anomaly.

Abortion Lawmakers: Moral Visionaries and Movement Politicians

I wanted to talk with the lawmakers. It seemed like the best way for me to understand what sort of expectations were behind this firestorm of new abortion laws. Did the legislators think the law could deter abortions? Were they persuaded that a speech from a doctor about fetal pain would cause some women to rethink their decisions? Or did they see the law as serving more symbolic purposes? Would they have agreed with Jordan of the Southern Baptist Convention, who said, "It may be tempting to postulate that the laws don't matter; that it's impossible to legislate morals. But no, you can legislate morality."

Although he had never held office, Lauinger's name was at the top of my list of people I wanted to interview. My conversations with Spiropoulos confirmed my sense that Lauinger played a central role in setting the state's antiabortion legislative agenda. Spiropoulos offered to call Lauinger on my behalf to tell him that I was "safe" and to ask him to meet with me.

When Lauinger didn't return my e-mails, I asked Spiropoulos if he'd reach out again. He did. Then, with only weeks to go before my visit, I left two voice messages at Lauinger's office. Finally, I found a residential listing under his name in Tulsa and left an apologetic message, introducing myself and all but pleading for the chance to meet him.

Mostly, I wanted to know what animates someone like him to devote his life to fighting to make abortion illegal. Pro-life men populate clinic protests, their red faces hurling epithets at cowering patients. But Lauinger didn't stand in the rain with a Bible and a placard. He was universally described as "courtly" and "gentlemanly."

To me, he seemed like the wizard behind the curtain. He was the unelected man who, from his home in the suburbs, waged a decades-long battle to change abortion law. And if victory was measured in numbers of laws passed, he seemed to be winning.

"Why the law?" I wanted to ask him. "What is it you believe will be changed when *Roe* falls?"

But Lauinger didn't return my calls or messages, so I never got to ask him. I learned later that, in addition to ignoring my entreaties, he also framed the scope of my interviews in Oklahoma. A week before my first visit to Oklahoma, Lauinger had sent e-mails to a long list of pro-life leaders around the state. One of the men I interviewed later read Lauinger's e-mail to me. Lauinger had written to him as an "ally," telling him that he and his assistant had declined my request to meet with them. He encouraged this man to do the same.

"She is pro-abortion," he wrote, and as proof, he included a link to an online petition I'd signed in 2007, decrying the threats to civil rights and to public health policy posed by forcing pregnant women to undergo testing for illegal drugs. He continued, "Long experience has taught me that there's nothing to be gained by helping gather intelligence from behind enemy lines from seemingly well-meaning academics." Now I understood why three Republican legislators had written to cancel our meetings, telling me they were too busy to reschedule.

In the end, I was left with a small but interesting cross-section of folks to interview. There were four former legislators and two sitting lawmakers, one who is widely viewed as the furthest right member in the State House of Representatives, and the other, the furthest left in the State Senate.

It was a rich pool in spite of Lauinger's interference. Two of the former lawmakers were pro-life Republicans; both had served for at least two terms and both had been in office during the recent shift in power. Because I wasn't looking to survey a large group of lawmakers, but rather to learn how they understood the role of law, the combined experiences and perspectives of those I interviewed proved to be plenty.

The Moral Visionary

Many of my interviews about abortion law in Oklahoma began with a preface, offered palms up and with an unwavering gaze: "I believe that abortion is the taking of a human life." If someone starts from that premise, it seems obvious why they would favor a complete ban on abortion. The law should not permit women to terminate their pregnancies any more than it should permit women to kill their two-week-old newborns. The law governing abortion should mirror the law governing homicide.

I went searching for a lawmaker who held these beliefs. I found State Representative Mike Reynolds.

Elected in 2002, Reynolds proudly told me that he's considered "the most outspoken member of the legislature."[14] He's passionate in his battle against the corruption he believes permeates much of state politics. He's crusaded against tax policies and other political stratagems that serve the interests of the four billionaires who "essentially control the whole state," including the newspapers and other media outlets that they own. That said, he is clear about what really matters to him.

"The stuff about corruption is games," he said. "The only thing I've ever cared about is saving unborn children."

I was a little surprised Reynolds still wanted to meet with me, given how many of his colleagues had canceled our interviews. "Ten o'clock will be perfect," he told me. "We can meet at H&H. That way, you can stay for lunch at the High Noon Club. It's every Friday. We have all sorts of speakers. Half the Republican caucus will be there, and sometimes the lieutenant governor and the governor come, too. The only rule of membership is, if you have to ask what time it meets, you can't come."

He laughed playfully and asked if I needed directions. I assured him I could find it on my own, and indeed, it was hard to miss. The H&H Shooting Sports store is like a small fluorescent city. It's home to the country's first National Shooting Sports Foundation's five-star indoor shooting range, which boasts thirty rifle lanes, twelve pistol lanes, and six air-gun lanes.

Reynolds met me at the door. A tall, fit man in man in his mid-sixties, he greeted me with twinkling eyes. Together, we passed through scores of aisles with shoulder-high shelves bearing crossbows, arrows, knives, shotguns, rifles, and pistols. An astonishing array of taxidermy stared down at me from various posts on the walls and atop the shelves— bears, large antlered deer, and smaller mammals, the names of which I must have learned in grade school.

"I've never been any place like this," I said, as we worked our way through the maze of weaponry. "And I've been to some pretty wild places."

"Thought so," he said, smiling.

Reynolds had first noticed the abortion issue in 1992, when the news covered the story of Dr. Nareshkumar Patel: "He was practicing, or murdering, in Warr Acres, Oklahoma. He was caught burning fetal remains in a Shawnee field. I organized a protest at his two clinics. And then I rented a 225-square-foot office in the same complex as his Shawnee clinic. We used it to intervene and counsel women going to Patel's clinic. I was dragged into legislative office ten years later because of my frustration with political corruption in the state, not because of abortion laws. The problem with abortion is more cultural than legal. Mothers and women are taught to see the unborn child as a thing. It's a cultural change that's needed, not a legal one. That doesn't mean that the pro-life movement won't do everything possible to change the law. But the culture also has to change."

"You were in office during this past decade," I noted, "when the state went from a Democratic to a Republican majority. Has that shift changed the way you view your job?"

"I'm not into coalition building," Mike responded. "I stand up for what I believe is right. I don't fight every battle, just the ones I run into." He laughed. "Seriously, though, I've only had five bills passed by the legislature in eleven years, and three of them were vetoed. I tend to spend my energy killing bad laws. I'm more afraid of doing the wrong thing than of not doing the right thing."

He went on: "The so-called pro-life movement is worried about pragmatics. Tony [Lauinger] takes slow, measured steps. He has his own sense of how to do things. Even though we both want the same outcome. . . . When I was first elected, Tony called me about a bill. He spoke for twenty-six minutes before he asked me what I thought. He's killed bills behind my back. And now, the Republican leadership has turned against me. They've cut me out of committee assignments. There are folks running against me, raising dirt about my past."

As Reynolds and I chatted, drinking water at H&H's 4U Café, our conversation veered into the personal. Reynolds spoke with remorse about things he'd done in his youth. There were tears, even though nothing he described struck me as unusual or even particularly blame-worthy. The difference was that over the course of time, he had developed a new sense of the meaning and purpose of his life. He regrets not having been a better person. And he lives now with the conscious intent to be the best person he can be.

Reynolds didn't go "off the record" with me when he spoke of his family, his faith, or his past. He is not a man who worries about the political implications of his personal beliefs.

He believes life begins at conception. He grieves that so many oral contraceptive users don't understand that the Pill doesn't merely prevent ovulation, but also stops a fertilized egg from implanting. I disagreed with him, explaining that the vast majority of hormonal contraceptives *do* work by suppressing ovulation so that the egg never ripens and there is nothing to fertilize, but he dismissed my interruption.

"I didn't know this fact until recently," he said. "It pains me enormously. It's why I supported the Personhood Act in both 2010 and 2012. Tony [Lauinger] argued against it this past term because he was afraid of failure. There were pro-business issues that worried the people from national, and they were calling the shots. Tony went to the Republican leadership and killed the bill. With Tony, it's always 'my way or the highway.'"

At high noon, we walked across the store to the paneled event room at the back. The stuffed animal heads gazed down from the walls, watching with feigned indifference. The room was already crowded when we arrived. The women all wore suits, as did around half of the men. The others wore flannel shirts and cowboy boots.

Reynolds steered me toward a tightly coiffed woman in her late fifties. "Hey Sally," he said, "I'd like to introduce you to Michelle Oberman."

Representative Sally Kern, who a week earlier had abruptly canceled our appointment, turned and took my hand. "Oh yes, I've heard your name. . . ." Suddenly she dropped my hand, her pink-lipsticked lips almost disappearing as she swung away from me.

The Pro-Life Movement Politician

I'll confess that I was as smitten as I was dumbfounded by my conversation with Reynolds. Like him, I aim to live in accordance with my moral compass. Like him, I feel badly when I fall short of the mark, which is often. Like him, I have a hard time understanding those whose lives seem out of sync with their professed moral sensibilities.

At the same time, I was troubled by his moral vision and, even more, by his willingness to use his office to impose it on others. He was convinced he had the truth, and he understood his election as a mandate to align the law with that truth. He had no patience for lawmaking by consensus and compromise. He was a political gadfly.

I gathered that the majority of his colleagues who had canceled their interviews with me belonged to what he termed "the so-called pro-life movement." And over the course of my time in Oklahoma, it became pretty obvious who controlled that movement.

Reynold's comments about the negative consequences of his rift with Lauinger over the Personhood Bill in 2012, when Lauinger changed his position and opposed the bill, weren't entirely surprising. He wasn't the only one to suggest that "with Tony, it's always 'my way or the highway.'" Nor was he the only one to allude to the power Lauinger had to influence which bills were introduced, whether they progressed, and even which legislators were denied key committee assignments. Or worse.

Former Democratic Representative Ryan Kiesel remarked that Lauinger could "use the fear of retribution in a way no one else can."[15] He recalled the 2010 debate over the Personhood Bill—the one that Lauinger supported, not the one he later lobbied against: "Tony sent letters to all the legislators saying that a vote against the bill would 'put their seat in jeopardy.'"

In spite of Lauinger's efforts to keep those in his pro-life network from talking with me, I found a solution in my interview with a former Republican legislator. He asked me not to use his name, so I'll call him Tom Smith.[16] Smith served over fifteen years in both the state House and Senate, and anticipates a run for higher office in the future. Hence, his desire for anonymity.

Smith ran for office on a job-creation platform, an interest he pursued over the long course of his career in public office. That said, Smith also noted that he is active in the Southern Baptist church. "I knew I was pro-life when I ran for office," he said. "I campaigned as such, and my voting record is perfect."

When I asked Smith how he understood the purpose of abortion law, his response was layered. The foundation was familiar: a core moral belief that abortion was murder, and a belief that the law should reflect this conviction. He said, "The purpose of the law is to stop abortion. To send a moral message. To get the message out via the law, to spark a debate in the population. The government's responsibility is to give people education. It is up to the government to tell them that abortion is wrong. It's not an acceptable solution."

Like Reynolds, Smith saw the law as somehow communicating to a hypothetical woman facing an unwanted pregnancy. The law sends her a message that abortion is wrong. But unlike Reynolds, Smith was a career politician. He had his own set of priorities that were unrelated to abortion. He was happy to show his loyalty to the pro-life cause by supporting the party's abortion agenda. He was able to list the issues, yet he had given little thought to the question of what might happen if the agenda actually became law. Indeed, I was struck by the lack of details in Smith's vision for what might happen if abortion became a crime.

Smith said the ideal replacement for *Roe* would be a law just like the one that existed in most states before *Roe*. (And, incidentally, just like the one that El Salvador had before the ban in 1998.)

"I'd favor making it a crime," he said, "but not under all circumstances. Maybe it would be banned entirely after the first twelve weeks. Or maybe it would allow abortion in the first twelve weeks only in cases of rape and medical necessity and fetal anomaly. And I think the doctors and the state would have to be serious about enforcing these exceptions. If a woman wanted an abortion on the grounds of rape, then they should make sure she actually filed criminal charges."

Yet Smith tossed out the alternatives as if they were interchangeable, like competing options in a political platform: "Make it a crime." "Keep it legal for the first twelve weeks." "Exceptions for rape." My sense that he was speaking in slogans, rather than actually thinking about how a change in abortion laws might work, was underscored by his list of the exceptions he'd permit to an abortion ban.

The list itself wasn't a surprise; he'd simply reverted to familiar old state laws. But the way he talked about closing the "maternal health exception" caught my attention. Many of the pro-life individuals I met talked about the need to close the maternal health loophole, inferring that, before *Roe*, women had obtained abortions by fabricating claims of mental distress or threatening suicide if they were denied an abortion.

I have not found any data confirming this claim, but I was struck by how often it was invoked over the course of my interviews in Oklahoma and elsewhere. It suggests the power of the pro-life movement to shape the imagination of its members, thereby dictating the terms of the legal landscape.

Lawmakers as Moral Messengers

For all their differences, what Reynolds and Smith had in common was a shared vision of the purpose of abortion law: the law is intended to make a moral condemnation. For example, here's how Smith responded when I asked him about why he would permit abortion at all, given his convictions: "What is it about rape that makes it OK for a woman to have an abortion? Do you see abortion as somehow less of a murder in those cases?"

"These exceptions reflect my value system," Smith explained. "'Judge not lest you be judged.' I'm OK with saying to a woman that abortion is wrong, but I'd leave room for a remedy in these cases."

Smith was far from the only person I met who spoke of an unwillingness to judge women who seek abortion under circumstances they viewed as extenuating. What interests me is the tacit willingness to pass judgment on women who seek abortion under all other circumstances.

Both Smith and Reynolds were relatively uninterested in my questions about the law's likely impact. When I asked Smith how abortion laws should punish violators, and about whether the law would actually deter abortion, these details struck him as secondary concerns. He was resigned to the idea that women would attempt to break the law.

"Well, I'd predict there would be a lot of girls and women who would travel," he said. "Those who could afford to would go someplace else. And there would be medicine abortions. It's hard to stop that from happening."

He seemed nonplussed by these shortcomings; the fact that some people would break the law was not a reason for legalizing the practice. From his perspective, the purpose of the law was to send a clear message about the wrongness of abortion.

MOVEMENT POLITICS AND
ABORTION'S LEGISLATIVE AGENDA

I learned three things when I asked people what would happen if *Roe* were reversed and abortion could once more be outlawed. The first was that the terms of the debate would likely be set by the pro-life movement, rather than by individual, impassioned lawmakers. The second was that those who identified as pro-life wouldn't yet have a consensus about how the law should look. Finally, I learned that this lack of consensus wouldn't stop the movement from demanding unwavering loyalty from its members.

Lauinger taught me each of these things.

Lessons from Lauinger

Due to Lauinger thwarting my efforts to meet with pro-life lawmakers, I learned that the pro-life movement in Oklahoma is run by elite outsiders, not by elected officials and not by community organizers. With a single e-mail, a never-elected activist could police the ranks of state officials against an outsider like me. More interesting was the way lawmakers anticipated that Lauinger and the Right to Life movement would shape the legislative agenda if *Roe* fell and abortion became a crime.

One of the questions I asked everyone I met was what they thought would happen in Oklahoma if *Roe v. Wade* fell.

Ryan Kiesel, who had served ten years in office fighting for reproductive rights, had a cynical response:

> The right doesn't want to win. They don't want *Roe* to fall. Opposing *Roe* is their template for running for office. It's their political touchstone. It avoids the need to talk about anything else. If that's taken away from them, they're going to have to deal with splits in coalition.[17]

Smith's prediction evoked similar concerns about fragmentation. "If *Roe* falls? I've honestly never considered it," he said. He paused for a moment, then added, "There'll be a huge fight on the right. The activists on the far right will want a complete ban, but the majority would want the exceptions I mentioned (rape, incest, life of the mother). The game of politics will dictate which exceptions make it into the law, because the control of special interests over this issue will be profound. It's not enough to please the 90 percent who identify as pro-life. You'll lose office because the 10 percent who are more extreme will organize to defeat you. That's what happened to Kris Steele."

Several of the people I interviewed in Oklahoma had mentioned former House Speaker Kris Steele in this tone, as if he'd somehow fallen from grace. Jordan of the Southern Baptist Convention invoked Steele as an example of a politician who was "maybe too collaborative," noting that he was "certainly seen to have been less reliable on pro-life issues." Democratic Senator Constance Johnson was more candid in her assessment. "Kris Steele had his lunch fed to him," she said, "because they didn't think he was conservative enough. He started to question Tony Lauinger. That was his sin."

Through the story of what happened to Steele I came to understand both the way in which pro-life movement elites set the agenda for lawmakers and the remorseless manner in which they punish those who deviate from the lockstep obedience they demand from members.

Kris Steele's Story

Former Oklahoma House Speaker Kris Steele's office is literally on the other side of the tracks, in an old brick building on the torn fringes of Oklahoma City. He runs an organization called The Education and Employment Ministry (TEEM). It provides job training, counseling, and housing for a lucky few of the hundreds of women who are released from Oklahoma prisons each year. Steele founded the nonprofit after he left office in 2012.

"We have the highest number of female inmates per capita in the world," Steele told me as he ushered me into the conference room, swinging his lame leg with grace. "They're here for drug-related crimes—theft, passing bad checks, all secondary to addiction," he said. "And there's a 70 percent re-incarceration rate for their children. But it's impossible to pass even evidence-based sentencing reform without being called soft on crime."[18]

I pulled out my papers. Steele asked if I'd mind if his intern joined us.

"I've been so eager to talk with you," he said, cutting off my introductory thank-you. "It's like *The Big Sort*, you know?"

Embarrassed, I confessed that I did not.

Steele was referring to Bill Bishop's book, *The Big Sort*, which describes the increased homogeneity of American communities over the past four decades—precisely the era since *Roe v. Wade* was decided. The provocative 2008 book called attention to the fact that we increasingly live in communities that reflect our values, places where we seldom encounter those who hold different viewpoints on core issues.

Bishop and others demonstrate the forty-year migration into value-segregated communities by tracking the number of counties that give landslide victories to either Democratic or Republication candidates. He begins with the 1976 election—a close race even at the county level—when just over 26 percent of American voters lived in counties that voted overwhelmingly for a particular candidate. By 2004, an equally divided electorate revealed a different pattern: 48.3 percent of Americans lived in "landslide" counties—places where the victors won by a margin of 20 percent or more. By 2012, over half of Americans lived in such communities.

The result, according to Bishop, is not simply a cultural sorting, but also an intensification of our differences. Citing research by social psychologists, he explains how, as people hear only their own beliefs reflected and amplified by those around them, they become more extreme in their thinking.

It suddenly hit me: I was as much a mystery to Steele and his intern as they were to me. How often did they meet someone who self-identified as a "liberal Democrat"? Somewhat self-consciously, I turned to my questions.

"Could you tell me about how you got involved with the abortion issue in Oklahoma?"

"As an ordained minister, my faith shapes my beliefs," Steele began.

I wondered when he became a minister; he looked no more than thirty years old.

"I'd been active in the pro-life movement prior to entering legislative service," he told me. "I was used to sharing my convictions, having lots of conversations, doing grassroots work on the issue."

"When did you join the House?"

"I was a representative from 2000 to 2012," he said, "and I served as speaker during the last two years. I was in the House when it turned Republican. You can skip most of your questions, I bet, because my record shows it: I'm a conservative, pro-life Republican."

"What was your goal in terms of abortion law reform?" I asked. "What sort of laws did you want to pass?"

Steele answered, "If you call a law *pro-life* in Oklahoma, it passes. No one has time to read all the bills, so the debate is reduced to, 'If you're pro-life, you'll support this bill.' Take the 'Safeguards for IVF' bill. It banned compensation for donating eggs. Somehow the money triggered fearmongering about women's exploitation, and we thought it was OK to bring the government into the lives of infertile couples. It was hard, in retrospect, to see how the bill was pro-life. Perhaps it was just pro-Catholic.

"It was my biggest regret in office—voting 'yes' on that bill," he added. "I only understood when one of my loyal constituents confided in me that his two precious children would not exist had they been unable to pay their egg donor."

"After that vote," Steele continued, "I realized the complexity of these issues and I started working for systemic change. I spent two years revamping Medicaid so it was a transparent, efficient, well-run program. It's the thing I feel most proud of."

I learned later, from those to Steele's right and left alike, that he'd responded to his constituent's story by campaigning against the 2010 in vitro fertilization bill in the State Senate. He succeeded, and the bill was voted down.

Steele left government in 2012, when he had reached the term limits, but my conversations with others suggested there was a more complicated story behind his departure.

One senior Republican lobbyist, speaking anonymously, tied Steele's fall from grace to the 2010 Personhood Act—the one Lauinger supported. "When Steele kept the 2010 Personhood Bill from reaching the House floor," he said, "he took the blame, even though the entire caucus voted with him."

Steele told me that out-of-state advocates had been pushing the 2010 Personhood Bill, wanting to use Oklahoma as a test case: "We already had a law saying life begins at conception. Why did we need one saying 'Constitutional rights attach at conception'? It's not possible to give the unborn the right to vote, so it seemed redundant to me."

In one of his final acts as House Speaker, Steele facilitated the 2010 Republican caucus's vote not to schedule the Personhood Bill for a hearing. He told me that the majority of the caucus had supported his decision to defer consideration of the bill, noting that it made sense in view of the proximity of the controversial vote to the general election. But in its aftermath, he alone took the blame for having scuttled the pro-life bill.

After the bill died, Steele said, "Church folk sent e-mails to me saying things like, 'I wish you'd never been born.'"

Lessons from Steele's Story

What are we to make of the way pro-life advocates regarded Steele's opposition to a single bill—one that the movement itself rejected in the very next legislative cycle—as a sign that he was not "reliably pro-life"?

The story sheds light on the ways in which single-issue advocates achieve their goals. It is a great example of what happens in state legislatures in response to many highly charged issues. Those who care most deeply are willing to invest time and money to influence their lawmakers. Those whose interests are more diffuse don't bother to raise their voices or to advocate loudly for a contrary position unless and until they too begin to care deeply about the issue.

It's called public choice theory, and it takes as its starting point the observation that, on any given issue, there are those who care deeply about it, and those who don't care as much. In the abortion context, those who are most motivated to make legislators hear their voices are those who believe that abortion is murder and should be banned. Their sense of urgency fuels the pro-life movement, giving it an outsized influence on the legislative process.

There's no real way to know whether their position on abortion is a majority view, but it turns out that that question is almost irrelevant. Their viewpoint will continue to hold sway until it offends the sensibilities of enough of those holding a contrary view that they, in turn, are prompted to mobilize in opposition. This phenomenon is precisely what Kiesel and Smith meant when they referred to the political battles likely to ensue should *Roe* fall.

I was amazed at how much admiration and heartache I felt for Steele. Amazed because his views on abortion were, at least in one sense, more extreme than anyone else I interviewed. He alone was comfortable endorsing the prosecution of women for abortion. "I'd expect there to be punitive consequences for blatant offenders of the law," he said, without hesitation. "Of course, I'd also incentivize carrying to term, but the core function of government is to protect its citizenry, so there must be consequences for those who break abortion laws."

What drew me in was the extent to which Steele expressed compassion for women facing an unwanted pregnancy. Smith had shrugged off the likelihood that women with enough money would evade the law by traveling. He seemed untroubled by the way the law would have a disproportionate impact on poor women. To him, the question of whether the law would stop abortions was almost beside the point.

Steele's response was different.

"Of course," he said, as we ended our conversation about abortion laws, "the best way to lower abortion rates is to deal with what causes women to want to abort in the first place."

Alone among the pro-life lawmakers and activists I met, Steele has direct experience working with poor women. Like the others, he wants the law to send the message that abortion is wrong. But only he seemed ready to acknowledge how little a change in the law will do to stop women from seeking abortions.

CONCLUSION

As I left Oklahoma that summer, I realized I'd learned a lot about the connection between morality, symbolism, and abortion laws. The message that abortion should be a crime was so pervasive that I suspected most Oklahomans no longer noticed it. At first I felt as though I couldn't escape it. It was on the billboards: "Abortion stops a beating heart." It was on the counter in the gym, where they sold Plexiglas photo key chains that said, "It's a life, not a choice" around the edges. It was there on the "I survived *Roe v. Wade*" bumper stickers on the trucks I passed on the highway.

After a while, I got used to the signs and the emblems. Images of fetuses became part of the landscape, like American flags or the crimson and cream of the University of Oklahoma Sooners. The pro-life messages were so ubiquitous that they faded into the background. But it's not a tranquil background. Instead, these messages generate an ominous sense that things are awry, and that it's on each of us to put them right again.

The mystery is how making abortion illegal will put things right. The battle over abortion law seems utterly disconnected from Steele's observation that "the best way to lower abortion rates is to deal with what causes women to want to abort in the first place." Doesn't everyone agree with him?

Oklahoma's ambitious body of abortion-restrictive laws is a testimony to the belief that the law matters. And if nothing else, the epic battle over abortion suggests that both sides share that belief: we take it for granted that changing abortion laws will change things in the lives of women facing unplanned pregnancies.

We've seen, both in El Salvador and in Oklahoma, how the law has become a vehicle for voicing moral opposition to abortion. And we've seen enough in El Salvador to know that banning abortion won't stop it from happening. We are now ready to investigate how and why abortion laws matter here in the United States.

The next chapter examines US abortion laws and policies, as well as those governing reproductive health care and motherhood in general. By illuminating the ways in which existing rules shape women's lives, we gain insight into how and how much abortion laws actually matter.

FOUR

THE ABORTION-MINDED WOMAN AND THE LAW

We've seen how abortion opponents have come to look at the law as a means of underscoring their belief that abortion is immoral. But the law is a tool; enforced, it has practical consequences. This chapter explores those consequences, considering the question of whether and how the law affects pregnant women who are considering abortion.

To think meaningfully about the issue, it helps to see the world through the eyes of such women. We must be clear about why a woman might consider having an abortion.

The largest research study into the question of why women choose abortion—it surveyed twelve hundred abortion patients—found most women cite not one, but several reasons: 74 percent said having a child would interfere with education, work, or their ability to care for dependents; 73 percent said they could not afford a baby now.[1]

The women are telling us something that is hiding in plain view: motherhood is really expensive. What's interesting about the costs of motherhood is that most of the costs actually could be reduced, if a government chose to do so. The price of being a mother is not foreordained. There is no "neutral" policy that dictates how much of the cost of mothering should fall on the individual mother. Instead, a country sets the price via a constellation of laws and policies: housing, day care, food, health care, education, and so on.

In order to understand how abortion laws work, we must also understand the impact of laws and policies that determine the costs of motherhood. You might picture a pregnant woman balanced on a scale, with abortion on one side and motherhood on the other. To understand the impact of changing the one side, you have to know what's on the other.

I knew I wanted to understand, up close, the sorts of things that really matter to women who are struggling over whether to terminate their pregnancies. The starting place for thinking about the laws and policies that influence women facing unwanted pregnancy was to spend time with those who are trying to influence actual women. This chapter begins with an extended interview with a group of pro-life advocates who think it's possible to sway those considering abortion. Indeed, they've spent the past four decades trying to do so.

After hearing their stories, the chapter considers the backdrop factors, economic and social, that might make a woman more or less inclined to carry a pregnancy to term. By examining these default norms, from child care to jobs and housing, we are able to see how the societal policies we take for granted shape the decisions of women facing unplanned pregnancy.

Then, with this background in mind, the chapter turns to an examination of the abortion laws and regulations enacted in the years since abortion became legal. Specifically, it considers the ways in which these laws and policies shift the balance, tilting women away from abortion.

In the end, we come away with a surprisingly clear, if troubling, sense of how the law can shape the decisions made by abortion-minded women.

LOBBYING AND LOVING THE ABORTION-MINDED WOMAN

One of the first organized responses of abortion opponents in the years following *Roe* was to open counseling centers that catered to women in "crisis" over an unplanned pregnancy. These centers aim to reach what they call "abortion-minded women," offering advice and varying degrees of support in the hopes of convincing a woman to carry her pregnancy to term.

There's a lot of controversy surrounding these centers. Abortion-rights advocates accuse them of false and misleading practices, like deliberately locating near abortion clinics or neglecting to mention that their center does not provide abortions or even abortion referrals. Pro-life advocates respond that they're enhancing women's choices by helping them find the support they need in order to keep their pregnancies. Even the name of these centers is controversial. Supporters call them "pregnancy care centers," while opponents employ the term historically used in the clinics' advertisements—"crisis pregnancy centers."

Regardless of the controversy, these faith-based counseling centers exist in far greater numbers than abortion clinics. Every day, they see women who are struggling in response to an unplanned pregnancy. And because they're endeavoring to persuade them not to have abortions, they know all about the things that make a woman consider having one.

Birth Choice of Oklahoma's main office is on the far south side of Oklahoma City. The red brick building sits alone on a stretch of a busy four-lane highway. Baby shrubs mark the lot's perimeter. With yellow Doric columns and three doorways topped with cheery porticos, it's like a mansion crossed with a strip mall.

I couldn't figure out which door was the entrance. The few cars in the otherwise empty lot were crowded near the smallest entrance, but there was no sign. Small piles of dirty snow flanked the sidewalk as I walked in the crisp March air. I approached the biggest door. Still no sign, but I peered through the glass window and saw a waiting room. A woman with long brown hair held her toddler in a worn armchair. She looked up, noticed my leather briefcase, my interview blouse and pearls, and glanced away as I raised my hand in a half wave.

When I had told people back home about my plan to visit a crisis pregnancy center, they'd joked about my needing a bulletproof vest. Would I pretend to be neutral, they'd wanted to know, or even pro-life?

I'd sent an e-mail to Barbara Chisko, the executive director, mentioning the names of two prominent pro-life advocates who had referred me to her: "I believe your long commitment to Birth Choice gives you a unique perspective on the law and its limitations, in terms of impacting women's responses to unplanned pregnancy."

Before I'd even explained my project, my background, and the questions I had, she wrote back, "Would love to meet with you." We spoke by phone and I think I said enough about why, as a law professor from California, I needed to travel to Oklahoma to better understand pro-life culture and its connection to the law. I didn't hide my position on legalized abortion, but later I wondered whether I'd been clear enough.

The young receptionist led me through a short hallway and across an empty dining room into a cozy pastel living room. Three women stood to greet me. I circled the group, shaking hands, smiling and saying my name, and took a seat on a soft floral sofa. A toddler with hair like corn silk sat on the floor across from me, playing with a plastic truck. The women looked at me expectantly.

"I want to thank you for being willing to meet with me," I said, hoping I seemed comfortable and relaxed. "It's hard to find people who will speak openly about abortion, and I come from such a blue state, if you know what I mean. I don't know very many people who are pro-life. And I don't know any pro-life activists."

"Let's begin by introducing ourselves," suggested Chisko, in the silence that had suddenly grown loud. Sitting in an armchair to my right, she pointed with her open palm to the pretty, spry woman who sat next to me on the couch.

In her late fifties, Katie Gordy was one of four Birth Choice founders. "I've done debates and abortion clinic confrontations for the Right to Life," she said. "But I hate all that. I'm a specialist in post-abortion counseling. I've been volunteering with Birth Choice since 1973. And I've been president of our board for the past fourteen years."

Rae Merchant walked into the room as Gordy was speaking. The drive down from the north-side clinic, which she's directed for thirty-four years, was slower than usual.

"I have eleven children," she offered when Gordy finished. "Eight are adopted and three are my biological kids. I've been a foster parent to 180 newborns. It all flows together for me," she said, lifting her hands and shrugging. "Adoption, foster care, parenting. That said, Birth Choice is my heart."

"It's because there's no shaming here," said Chisko. "No judgment. Women come in and we love on them. No shame, just love." She laughed.

"I think people connect in their brokenness," Gordy added quietly, looking down.

"I'm doing pregnancy tests now on women whose mothers I helped years ago," said Merchant. "We listen with a nonjudgmental ear. We work on offsetting this quick-fix society. We help them understand that abortion won't fix things."

It was the first time I'd heard the term "quick-fix society," but I didn't need a translation. I thought about the women I'd met in the Ohio Reformatory for Women when I was studying mothers who killed their children. My coauthor and I had asked them why they hadn't terminated their pregnancies. The chaos in their lives was profound and long-standing. They must have known a new baby would make their lives even harder.

"My family doesn't believe in abortion. That's murder," many replied without irony. Indeed, most hadn't intentionally killed their children. Instead, their babies' deaths were almost predictable by-products of their grim circumstances.

"I know what you mean about the quick fix," I said, and told them about the mothers I'd met in prison.

Typically when I speak about their crimes, I can sense the disgust these mothers evoke in others. Their situations may have been terrible, but their crimes seem too heinous to merit sympathy, let alone empathy.

The women all started to speak at once.

"I suspect the majority of those women may have had previous abortions," said Chisko.

Merchant offered a different theory, saying, "I've observed in my work with women who abuse their children that a lot of them wanted to have kids, but then their kids failed to meet their expectations."

From across the room, Ellen Roberts spoke for the first time. Sitting on the floor next to her small son, Roberts was at least twenty years younger than the rest of us. She tucked her chin-length chestnut hair behind an ear and said, "Working here, I've learned that it's not their bad choices that have landed the women at our door, but rather God's grace that kept me from being in their situations."

Conversation began to flow as the personal merged with the professional. We all had stories to share.

A woman in a pink polo shirt walked into the living room, calling, "Time for lunch, ladies."

She walked over to me. "Hi, I'm Ruth Blakely," she said, extending a firm hand. "Another one of the four founders. Nice to meet you."

We moved into the dining room, taking seats around the big square table. From the galley kitchen tucked behind the far wall, another woman stepped out to join us.

"This is my daughter and our accountant," said Chisko, with a broad smile.

With Roberts's son in his highchair, we were eight in all. Without hesitation, I bowed my Jewish head as Chisko said grace.

With the exception of Roberts and Barbara's daughter, these women all were veterans of 1973. Each dated her entry into pro-life activism to learning, in church, that abortion had been legalized.

"I couldn't believe that women would tear apart their own babies. Or that they could be coerced into doing so," said Chisko. "You know, doctors have a way of telling women what they think is best. And our clients . . ."

"People judge our clients," Merchant interrupted. "Especially those on welfare. 'Why do these women keep having babies?' they ask. The common denominator is the desire to be loved. Even a 'lowlife' wants to be loved. We all crave intimacy."

"The four of us met at a church event," Chisko began, sitting back in her chair. "We signed up to volunteer with the Right to Life. They suggested we put ads in the paper for 'crisis pregnancies.' But they left after four months, leaving us with one phone line and a folding chair.

"We offered a training session for volunteer counselors and a hundred and eighty people showed up. But only twenty stayed on as regular volunteers. We just didn't know what we were doing. We had a burning desire to help people, to meet them where they are. I myself had just had a miscarriage. At that time, pro-life simply meant 'don't murder your baby.' We felt our job wasn't to evangelize or proselytize. Just live life as you should. Be a model. At first, we were part of 'Birth Right,' an international group. But by the 1980s, the organization set rigid rules: no shelters, no clinical services, just administer pregnancy tests and give out baby clothes. Just persuade the women not to abort their babies."

"They like to shame women," said Merchant. "In Lawton's clinic, they have a life-size cardboard Jesus in the lobby."

"Birth Choice's priorities are shaped by the belief that the best place for a child is with mom," Chisko added.[2]

I was beginning to understand what Roberts had meant when she'd said, earlier that morning, that there were "two kids of pro-life people. People who are pro-life and people who are antiabortion."

"The antiabortion folks are really difficult to work with," Roberts remarked. "They use our clients to fight their fight. But they never come to fight our fight."

The women's passion for supporting the poor surprised me. I thought social conservatives typically blamed the poor for not working harder to change their circumstances. It was the Democrats who supported welfare, minimum wage laws, and a bigger safety net. Yet these women, like everyone else I'd met in pro-life Oklahoman circles, were Republicans.

I didn't really know whether they were exceptions to the norm among social conservatives, though, because I couldn't remember the last conversation I'd had with a social conservative.

"How did Rose Home come to be?" I asked. Several of the pro-life religious and political figures I'd interviewed had mentioned Birth Choice's shelter for pregnant women.

"It was through an adoption agency referral, back in our crisis pregnancy clinic in 1986," said Chisko, setting her fork down. "The woman had had several prior pregnancies that ended in abortion or adoption. She'd planned to relinquish her current pregnancy, but slowly she changed her mind."

Chisko sighed and looked at Gordy, Merchant, and Blakely, shaking her head and smiling. "She needed help parenting and she needed money. The adoption agency billed her thousands of dollars when she pulled out. Volunteers made it work. An attorney friend of ours made the bill go away. When this woman spoke at our twenty-fifth-anniversary dinner, she thanked us. 'You taught me how to trust,' she said."

Chisko's voice cracked and her eyes were wet.

Gordy continued for her, "At first, we tried to serve our clients by finding them jobs and housing. But our clients weren't always well received."

"There were some angel donors for Rose Home," Chisko said, gesturing around the room, which could comfortably have held another three dining tables.

"We opened Rose Home in 1986," she continued. "We've had a woman stop in at thirty-five weeks' gestation. Terrified of the health-care system. A twelve-year-old girl in foster care was gang-raped. She was being pushed by the state to have an abortion. She didn't want it, so I helped arrange to take her into federal jurisdiction, where a federal judge gave Birth Choice custody of her. We brought her home and eventually we helped her get money so she could be reunited with her mom and move to a safer neighborhood."

The story rang a bell. It had gotten a lot of national press. I remember cringing at the thought of how a twelve-year-old rape victim had been manipulated into carrying to term. I didn't share this memory with the women.

Only later did I wonder why I was so sure this twelve-year-old girl I didn't know would have been better off having an abortion than carrying to term.

———————

Roberts described how Rose Home chooses its residents:

> We see three hundred to four hundred women a month here at Birth
> Choice, plus another hundred or so at the north-side clinic. We
> do blood workups, check blood pressure and weight. We help the
> women get covered by Sooner Care and make prenatal referrals to
> St. Anthony's. If they're ineligible for insurance, we provide their
> prenatal care.
>
> Some of our clients are struggling with domestic violence, or
> they're couch surfing or living out of a car. We screen for these issues
> and offer housing to those who truly have no place else to go. We can't
> accept severely mentally ill clients, which is a real problem. There's
> nowhere to send these women. They have to be violent before they
> qualify for housing in a state group home. But we can't handle them
> at Rose Home.

Because many of the women are fleeing violent relationships, the
shelter's location is undisclosed. They can bring their children with
them, so long as they are under age five.

The residents almost always qualify for public assistance, which
helps with funding. In weekly meetings with their caseworkers, the
women articulate goals and plan their futures. They receive mental
health counseling, drug abuse treatment, and vocational training. They
get help making court dates, as many have open cases for abuse and
neglect. There are quarterly meetings and ongoing support services even
after they leave Rose Home.

"How many women live in Rose Home?" I asked.

"We can house five women at a time. And up to thirteen children,"
Roberts answered.

"Doesn't it break your heart, having to turn away so many needy
women?" I asked no one in particular.

"It's cheaper to have an abortion than to have a baby," Merchant said.

"There's no doubt that the bottom line encourages abortion," Chisko added. "Even though there aren't enough young people to pay for older people. Dr. Wilke's *Handbook on Abortion* spotted this issue, as did Paul Marx's *The Death Peddlers*," Chisko continued. "And it's true. The majority of our clients need food and clothes. But they're not at Birth Choice for resources. They come because we help them feel worthy, cared for, and trusted."

The rhetoric was new to me. I hadn't thought about the way the high costs of raising a child are an incentive for abortion. It's so obviously true.

Don't get me wrong—the long interview wasn't entirely a "kumbaya" moment, as we say in my family. Some of the things said left me stunned in disbelief. Like when Merchant said, "So many of our ills—violence in the world, weather phenomena, Obamacare—are all tied to abortion."

When I asked whether they would support a complete ban on abortion, telling them briefly about Beatriz's case, Chisko answered without hesitation: "I learned early on that if a woman is healthy enough to get pregnant, she's healthy enough to go to term." She recalled a woman with a heart condition who'd been advised to terminate. The woman had refused, and according to Chisko, she had her baby and is alive today.

She believed that Beatriz did not need an abortion to survive. Indeed, she sees Beatriz's survival as proof of her point.

But when it came time to say goodbye, I mostly felt awed by what I'd witnessed there. The women of Birth Choice had aligned their moral compasses with a keen eye to the needs of the most vulnerable women in society. I loved them for it.

"If the law changes," I asked, "If *Roe* falls and abortion becomes illegal, will Birth Choice still be here?"

"We'll be here no matter what," Chisko answered. "Women are always going to get pregnant and they're always going to struggle."

DEFAULT NORMS: THE CONTEXT IN WHICH
U.S. WOMEN MAKE ABORTION DECISIONS

One of the most important things I learned from the women at Birth Choice was to view the decision to keep or to end a pregnancy from the perspective of a woman struggling to decide. In order to understand the impact of abortion laws, we must first consider the backdrop against which such decisions take place. That backdrop is easiest to see when one focuses on the experience of the most vulnerable women. The women at Rose Home.

Of course, the backdrop is there for everyone, not just for poor women, and not just in the context of abortion. There are norms and policies that shape and constrain our options in life. The backdrop norms informing decisions about abortion consist of our policies regarding motherhood and parenting. We mostly regard these policies as neutral. But when we see their impact on the most vulnerable women, we understand how one's circumstances circumscribe the "choices" one actually has.

What Makes a Woman Consider Abortion?

"What makes a woman consider having an abortion?" I asked Samara Azam-Yu, executive director of Access Women's Health Justice in Oakland, California.

"Women have been making hard choices forever," she answered. She works with the poorest women in the state, helping them arrange travel from small towns throughout northern and central California to San Francisco in order terminate unwanted pregnancies.

> There are people who spend their life savings, travel hundreds of miles to get procedures, and then don't even have the money to get home. California has the highest poverty rate in the US. The economy crashed in 2008, and years later, the people I serve are running on fumes. Abortion is not really a "choice" for the women who call us for help. A baby will push the family deeper into poverty.

After seven years of working with women living on the thin edge of despair, Azam-Yu has almost as little patience for the rhetoric of "choice" as she does for that of "life." The way she sees it, abortion decisions arise out of desperation.

Azam-Yu said, "There's a Native American nurse at an abortion clinic in San Francisco who put it this way. She said, 'If you have twins and it's a bad year, you have to put one in the badger hole.'"

Until I met both Azam-Yu and the women at Birth Choice, I hadn't realized the extent to which, by thinking and talking about abortion in hypothetical terms—the rape victim, the unwed teenager, the fetus with Down syndrome—we distort reality. We erase the complex network of factors underlying a woman's decision to end her pregnancy.

A woman faces the surprise of an unplanned pregnancy as if on the tracks, with a locomotive barreling toward her. The only variation lies in how many other trains are coming at her from other directions.

Azam-Yu and the Birth Choice founders see the most vulnerable women in society, the ones who, even before they got pregnant, spent their days trying to avoid incoming trains—housing, food insecurity, abusive relationships, addiction.

Azam-Yu told the story of a client she'd recently helped:

> One woman came by bus from Arcata, in the far north of the state. She found someone to watch her kids for two days. Access Women's Health Justice paid for the six-hour bus ride to San Francisco. Found her a place to stay the night. One of our volunteers drove her to the UCSF clinic. She got there, and was meeting with the pre-abortion counselor. After around half an hour she said, "I'm so sorry. I've changed my mind. Now that I've had time to think about it . . ."

Azam-Yu's work with Access Women's Health Justice has one approach to helping poor women resolve unplanned pregnancies. Birth Choice has another. Their clients are one and the same, though. So many things weigh on these women as they confront their pregnancies that it's hard to know how best to help them.

"There's so much chaos in our clients' lives," Azam-Yu said, after telling me about the woman who'd changed her mind about having an abortion, "that choices aren't real until they are actually confronted with them."

I want us to bear this woman in mind as we consider the way laws and policies set the ground rules and expectations for motherhood. She helps make visible the ways in which our policies about motherhood set the context in which women respond to an unplanned pregnancy.

Motherhood's Default Norms

Think back to Chisko's observation that "the bottom line encourages abortion." She was calling attention to the costs associated with having a child. When asked their reasons for seeking abortion, women make reference to many such costs. Work, school, ability to care for others, and money—each factor is affected by policies; each reflects governmental priorities. Consider an obvious example: there is no paid maternity leave in the United States. And there's no subsidized day care. Yet the majority of women in the country must work in order to support their households. These policies reflect a position that the costs of caring for children are a private responsibility, rather than a public obligation.

These policies seem neutral. But upon reflection, and certainly from the perspective of the most vulnerable women, we can understand these policies as reflections not only of governmental priorities, but also as factors that influence whether poor women will opt to have children.

In many countries worldwide, including most of Western Europe, governments pay families a monthly allowance for each child they are raising. Day care is affordable, as is health care. Both are government subsidized. Workers are guaranteed several months paid maternity leave. In some countries, mothers receive a year off from work, with pay, after having a baby. These policies are meant to encourage child-bearing over abortion by offsetting the costs of having a child. These countries want more children.

Like Western Europe with its child allowances, the United States has a fertility policy. We know how much it costs to have a baby; we know how much it costs to raise a child. And for the most part, we refuse to subsidize that cost.

You might argue that we're simply remaining neutral, allowing families to make their own private decisions about when and whether to have children. But what is the place from which "neutrality" is measured?

Let me make my point clear by telling you about California's fertility policy. Like many states, until 2016, California had a "family cap" law as part of its welfare provisions.[3] If you have a child within the first year after enrolling, you don't get any additional support from the state.

Lawmakers around the country from both political parties support family caps as necessary disincentives for women who otherwise might have babies simply to increase their monthly income. Former president Ronald Regan called them "welfare queens," and for almost forty years, the fear of lazy women having babies in order to live off the social dole has animated our collective imagination. Their choices seem like a form of reproductive blackmail.

Azam-Yu's organization, Access Women's Health Justice, waged a ten-year battle against California's family caps. She recalled one of its former clients, Melissa Ortiz, who testified in a legislative hearing about the impact of the cap on her family. Ortiz was supporting four children on just $516 a month in aid:

> When we first had the twins, the only person in my family getting aid was my oldest son. We didn't have money to buy them car seats to get home [from the hospital]. . . . We didn't have money to pay for diapers, wipes, shampoos, and toiletries. . . . I had to go to charities, wait in line, and hope that the charities had diapers that day. . . . I am constantly trying to pay just enough to not have [the utilities] shut off. . . . I am trying my best to be a great mom. I do not need to be punished for deciding to have children.[4]

In an era of bitter partisan animosity, family caps enjoy rare bipartisan support. In spite of the enormous wealth separating the United

States from countries like El Salvador, US mothers like Ortiz have to ration their babies' diapers in much the same way that I witnessed in El Salvador.

Having a baby in the United States is expensive. And the government is comfortable with the high price point.

"No one who's at all savvy will say they don't want poor women to have children, because that sounds eugenic," Azam-Yu said. "But they will say, 'There's no money in the budget for that.'"

I don't mean to suggest that only poor women struggle when confronted with an unplanned pregnancy, or that money is the only factor that shapes a woman's response. Instead, I have described their struggles because they are so basic that they make it easy to see how policy choices (not to subsidize maternity leave, housing, day care, or even diapers) constrain American women's mothering choices.

Once we recognize the costs of having children as constraints on motherhood, we can more readily see the context in which all women find themselves when facing an unplanned pregnancy. If we broaden the lens now to include all women, rather than only the poorest women, we can see the ways in which women who are better off have more options. Without a doubt, as we move up the socioeconomic ladder, these backdrop policies have less force. If she has a good job, a place to live, a strong relationship, or family ties, a woman has options, even if the government does not offset the costs of having a child.

A woman whose basic needs are met has time to think about her options. She can consider her best response to the train coming down the tracks. This does not mean that the train ceases to exist, though.

Abortion is not the result of a simple yes/no calculus. Rather, it's the product of weighing competing costs. On one side of the scale are the costs of motherhood. On the other are the costs associated with abortion—costs that are largely determined by the legal regulations and restrictions on abortion.

REGULATING ABORTION:
HOW DO ABORTION LAWS WORK?

In order to understand how the law shapes the cost of abortion, it is important to recognize the significance of both criminal laws and civil laws and regulations. The Supreme Court's 1973 decision in *Roe v. Wade* barred states from making it a crime to have an abortion before viability. It left states free to regulate abortion, though, just as they would any other health procedure. And they did.

Abortion Laws as Nudges and Shoves

When the US Supreme Court determined that women had a constitutional right to abortion, and that states could not make abortion a crime, the Supreme Court tipped the balance away from motherhood and toward abortion. Before the decision, abortion was illegal in forty-eight states. After, it was legal in fifty. The law changed the balance; once abortion became legal, it became easier for women to choose abortion over motherhood.

Pro-life lawmakers have been working to tip the balance back ever since.

Behavioral economists talk about the complicated ways laws can influence human behavior, creating incentives or disincentives that cause humans to alter their default course of action.[5] Professor Dan Kahan describes how lawmakers try to shape human behavior by drafting laws that operate as either "gentle nudges" or "hard shoves."[6]

As an example, he cites the way the law responded to the alarming findings of the 1964 surgeon general's report, which for the first time linked smoking to cancer. Rather than banning smoking, which would have generated intense conflict because so many Americans smoked cigarettes, the law proceeded with gentle nudges: first, it included warning labels on packages; then the law banned cigarette advertisements on television. Only decades later, after the norms regarding smoking had shifted, did the law employ a "hard shove" by banning smoking in public areas.[7]

To understand how abortion laws work, we might see them as ways of nudging or shoving a woman toward or away from abortion. The very first congressional battle over abortion after *Roe* was decided is a great example of how abortion laws are intended to shift the balance—to nudge the pregnant woman away from abortion and toward motherhood.

Congress passed the Hyde Amendment in 1976, prohibiting the use of federal dollars for abortions, except in cases of rape, incest, or medical necessity.[8] The law was important for symbolic reasons: abortion opponents didn't want their tax dollars to be spent on abortion. But lawmakers also saw in the law an opportunity to tip the balance away from abortion. Here's how Representative Henry Hyde explained his law's goals: "I certainly would like to prevent, if I could legally, anybody having an abortion: a rich woman, a middle-class woman or a poor woman. Unfortunately, the only vehicle available is the . . . Medicaid bill."[9]

It worked. Researchers later demonstrated the impact of restricting federal funding. They studied abortion rates between 1974 and 1988, examining what happened when the federal government and some states banned taxpayer funding for most abortions. When states denied public funding, they saw a 5 percent decline in abortion rates.[10] The impact of denying funding is particularly stark among the poorest women. The study found that, without funding, 22 percent of abortions that would otherwise have occurred did not take place. By refusing to pay for poor women's abortions, a state can get thousands of women to have babies instead of abortions.

In the first twenty years following *Roe*, states with pro-life majorities explored other ways of using abortion regulations to tip the balance away from abortion. They passed laws requiring pregnant teens to obtain parental consent, and laws requiring patients to wait a day or two between requesting an abortion and actually getting one.[11] Proponents saw the regulations as responsive to state goals of protecting health and life. Opponents decried the laws as obstacles to a woman's ability to exercise her constitutional right. Legal battles ensued in almost every state as lawmakers tested the limits of their power to regulate abortion.

Eventually, the Supreme Court had to resolve the disputes by letting states know how far they could go in their attempts to nudge women away from abortion. In 1992, the Supreme Court decided *Planned Parenthood v. Casey*, creating the "undue burden test":[12]

> Unless it [imposes an undue burden] on her right of choice, a state measure designed to persuade her to choose childbirth over abortion will be upheld if reasonably related to that goal. Regulations designed to foster the health of a woman seeking an abortion are valid if they do not constitute an undue burden.[13]

For pro-life lawmakers, *Casey*'s "undue burden" test was an invitation to pass laws intended to dissuade abortion-minded women. At first, pro-life states moved slowly, with most states focusing on issues like waiting periods. Starting in 2004, the pro-life group Americans United for Life launched a model legislation project. It drafted a broad set of antiabortion laws, including provisions banning abortion after twenty weeks on the grounds that the fetus could feel pain, and restricting the settings and the providers for abortions. The group encouraged pro-life states to enact whole slates of antiabortion laws, keeping track of its successes with a national pro-life "report card" system.

Some of these model statutes are plainly unconstitutional, as they have the effect of completely curtailing abortion. One state, for instance, passed a law revoking the medical license of any doctor performing an abortion.[14] But most of the laws work at the margins—nudging rather than shoving women away from abortion.

How Much Do Abortion Laws Tip the Balance?

There is surprisingly little consensus about whether and how much these abortion laws and regulations matter. We simply don't know how often laws requiring things like waiting periods or ultrasounds tip the balance, leading a woman to choose to carry to term rather than abort her pregnancy.

At the national level, there's a bitter dispute about whether restrictive abortion laws lead to lower rates of abortion. Since 2008, abortion rates have been declining all over the country.[15] The leading pro-life economist says this decline proves the laws are working to deter women from having abortions. The pro-choice economists respond that he's wrong, because abortion is declining throughout the country, including in states without pro-life laws.[16]

For our purposes, though, the question is not necessarily how often or how much the laws deter abortion. What we want to know is how the law might tip the balance away from abortion.

Sociologist Sarah Roberts has undertaken a deep inquiry into how abortion restrictions affect women's actual decisions. After Utah enacted a seventy-two-hour waiting period, one of the longest in the country, Roberts surveyed five hundred women who sought abortions in Utah. Her study found that the waiting period had an impact on women's decisions, but in a surprisingly indirect manner:

> The 72 hour waiting period and two-visit requirement did not prevent women from having abortions, but it did burden women with financial costs, logistical hassles, and extended periods of dwelling on decisions they had already made. The wait also led some women to worry that they would not be able to obtain abortion drugs, and pushed at least one beyond the clinic's gestational limits for abortion.[17]

Roberts found no evidence suggesting that the three-day waiting period led women to change their minds about abortion. But it is clear that the law had an impact on the woman contemplating abortion: it increased the costs of having an abortion.

Laws restricting abortion by banning insurance coverage or requiring waiting periods don't target any particular set of pregnant women. The laws are neutral on their face. Yet poor women disproportionately feel the impact of these laws.

Take, for example, a hypothetical low-income single mother in Wisconsin. In recent years, that state enacted a law requiring a twenty-four-hour waiting period, and another law banning the use of telemedicine by abortion providers. The state has only three abortion providers, all in Madison or Milwaukee. The abortion procedure itself costs, on average, $593. For a single mother in rural Wisconsin, though, the actual costs are much higher. To the cost of the procedure, she must add the costs triggered by the waiting period and the distance she must travel. Gas, lodging, child care, and missed work add up, so that in the end, an abortion actually costs her $1,380.[18]

In the end, abortion laws aim to nudge women away from abortion by raising the costs of getting one. And the women most likely to be nudged away from abortion because of the costs are those who are poor. Ironically, and to my mind most cruelly, these are the same women who were nudged toward abortion because of the high costs of motherhood.

Our policies on both ends of the scale leave poor mothers so constrained by their options that it is hard, in good faith, to see either motherhood or abortion as a "choice."

CONCLUSION

From a distance, we can see that the abortion laws in the United States are not different in kind from those in El Salvador. El Salvador's ban on abortion works by raising the costs and risks associated with terminating a pregnancy. Wealthier girls and women in El Salvador are better able to offset these costs; they have access to private doctors, and they can travel. They are more insulated than their poorer sisters from the hard shove of the abortion ban.

Likewise, US policies and regulations governing motherhood and abortion are simply ways of pushing a woman one way or the other as she contemplates her response to an unplanned pregnancy. There's the dramatic push of making abortion legal (or criminal). And there are the gentle pushes offered by the Birth Choice women. No life-size cardboard Jesus to shame them. Instead, perhaps, a life rope. Health insurance, housing, help finding work, the prospect of being reunited with children lost to foster care.

The behavioral economists speak of nudges and shoves, distinguishing laws that work indirectly and gradually (the nudges) from those that directly penalize a given activity (the shoves). But when it comes to abortion, this dichotomy between nudges and shoves does not fully capture the impact of the law on pregnant women. Not all nudges are alike. Or rather, what feels to one woman like a gentle nudge is a hard shove to another.

Let's be honest about our abortion policies. Rather than nudging a poor pregnant woman by giving her incentives to choose motherhood, contemporary US abortion laws work by constricting her options. Whether for reasons of fiscal constraint or a belief that abortion is morally abhorrent, our antiabortion laws are cheap. They show no love for the abortion-minded woman. Instead, they work to tip the scales toward childbirth by simply raising the costs of abortion.

The real challenge for abortion laws is yet to come. Pro-life lawmakers cannot be content with laws that merely nudge women toward childbirth or away from abortion. They've been elected on a platform that affirms that life begins at conception and regards abortion as murder.

There is a pent-up demand for the harder shove of making abortion illegal.

The final chapter of this book examines the changes that will be set in motion in the event that *Roe* is reversed and states are once again free to make abortion a crime.

FIVE

AMERICA AFTER *ROE*

Of the many things dividing the United States, none seems more salient than the divide between pro-life and pro-choice forces. At the heart of the dispute is an assumption that, if *Roe* is reversed and abortion becomes illegal, things will change.

We talk about banning abortion as if we all understand how things will change if abortion becomes a crime. On both sides, we invoke naive generalities and obsolete references when imagining post-*Roe* America. The coat hangers, staple features of pro-choice protesters, suggest that women will die if abortion becomes illegal. And the pro-life slogan, "Stop abortion now," seems to assert that making abortion illegal will stop women from having them.

These vague suggestions do not serve us well. Rather, they impede clear thinking about what will happen if states are permitted to make abortion illegal. A variety of legal issues will be set in motion by permitting states to criminalize abortion, many of which arise from the fact that, even without *Roe*, abortion will remain legal in many states around the country.

After considering how *Roe*'s demise would alter, but not halt, women's access to legal abortion in the United States, I turn to the issue of abortion law enforcement. Making abortion a crime is actually more a question than an answer. If abortion is a crime, who are the criminals?

As we reflect upon the way in which laws against abortion matter, the experiences of other countries have much to teach us. You already know a good deal of these lessons, having taken this journey with me. You'll remember Beatriz, whose illness and doomed fetus illuminated the ways in which symbolic laws get tested by hard facts. You've met Christina and the other Salvadoran women serving long prison sentences for crimes they did not commit.

Questions of abortion law enforcement are clear: who will we target for punishment, and who will we actually catch? The choices we face, as we look to abortion crimes, are surprisingly obvious, and the consequences are as disturbing as they are predictable.

ABORTION LAWS IN THE ABSENCE
OF A CONSTITUTIONAL RIGHT

Judging from how we fight over *Roe*, you might think that if *Roe* were overturned, it would be impossible to get a safe, legal abortion in the United States. The truth is otherwise: those with enough time and money will find it easy to obtain a legal abortion, regardless of the laws in their home state. This is because abortion will remain legal in many US states, regardless of the Supreme Court's position on the matter.

Let me explain. Back in 1972, every state had its own laws about abortion. Most states made it a crime, but included some exceptions, such as in cases where the mother's life or health was at risk. A few states—New York, Washington, California, and Hawaii—had recently legalized abortion, permitting it for any reason, before viability. Rather than "legalizing" abortion, the Supreme Court's 1973 decision in *Roe* effectively told the other forty-six states they needed to do so, too.

Talk about the law making a hard shove! By finding that a woman has a constitutional right to privacy under the Fourteenth Amendment, the court overturned the criminal laws of forty-six states.[1] Any decision that reverses *Roe* must begin with a reconsideration of the scope of the constitutional right to privacy.

Roe v. Wade used the concept of fetal viability as the outer limit on a woman's right to privacy. A woman has a broad right to abortion, as a matter of her private choice, before the point at which the fetus is viable. If the fetus is not yet capable of living outside the woman's body, abortion is permissible. If the fetus could survive independently, however, she can no longer abort it.

There was no axiomatic reason for picking viability as the dividing line, though. The court might just as easily have drawn the line earlier or later in pregnancy. And in the absence of *Roe*, a state might well choose some other cutoff point along the gestational path. Indeed, several states have passed laws banning abortion any time after one can hear a fetal heartbeat. Although these laws cannot currently take effect because *Roe* still protects a woman's constitutional right to abortion, they hint at how some states might want to restrict abortion if *Roe* falls.

Even if the Supreme Court reverses itself and decides that the Constitution no longer protects a woman's right to abortion, though, it still will need to set limits on how states frame their abortion laws. For example, it is clear that no state could ban abortion completely. No state could force a woman to continue a pregnancy that poses a threat to her life because the Constitution guarantees a woman's right to life. Unlike in El Salvador, where the country's constitution declares a right to life from the moment of conception, nothing in our Constitution recognizes an absolute "right to life" for the fetus. And there's little chance of this changing any time soon: Constitutional amendments are exceptionally hard to pass, requiring approval not just by both houses of Congress, but also ratification by a majority vote in three-quarters of the states in the country.[2]

If the Supreme Court reverses *Roe*, then, the open question is how far the court will allow states to go. Will it narrow a woman's privacy right to some earlier point in pregnancy, or will it jettison the privacy right altogether, permitting states to dictate the circumstances under which abortion will be allowed?

It's worth playing out the tape on the most extreme case, just to see how much it would matter. Let's imagine that the Supreme Court goes so far as to permit states to ban abortion except when a woman's life is at risk. How many states would subsequently enact such bans?

When I asked a pro-life Oklahoman state senator what would happen if *Roe v. Wade* were reversed, he sighed and said, "It will be a bloodbath on the right." Pro-life communities will be forced to reckon with the disparate views of their constituents, the vast majority of whom want to keep abortion legal in cases of rape, incest, and fetal anomaly. If *Roe* falls, there will be a furious battle over how to frame the crime of abortion.

But not all states will be fighting. Perhaps the most important thing to remember when thinking about America after *Roe* is that not all states will choose to criminalize abortion. Even without *Roe*, abortion will remain legal in as many as half the states. This fact often gets lost in the contentious debates over the Supreme Court's rulings on abortion. In a number of states around the country, the Supreme Court position doesn't make a difference. Many states are safely pro-choice, with judicial decisions interpreting state constitutions as protecting a woman's right to privacy, and large majorities favoring legalized abortion.[3]

If *Roe v. Wade* is reversed, it is clear that the battle over abortion laws will not end. Instead, while pro-life states struggle to determine the scope of laws restricting abortion, elsewhere, abortion will be legal. As a result, it is fair to say that the most significant barrier to abortion, in a world without *Roe v. Wade*, will be wealth: how much will an arbortion cost and how far must one travel in order to get one?

ACCESS TO LEGAL ABORTION IN A POST-*ROE* AMERICA

We already know what happens when abortion becomes a crime. Women with money get abortions by traveling to places where it is legal. Remember what I told you about Chile, where I met Marina, who told me, "The rich women fly to Miami. Women like me stay here."[4]

"Abortion tourism," as it is known, happens here, too. In 1972, the year before *Roe*, when abortion was legal in only four states, a review of medical records shows that 40 percent of abortions were performed on women who came from out of state.[5] Even today, when abortion is legal in all fifty states, women travel in order to avoid local abortion restrictions. For example, in 2014, New Mexico's Department of Health data revealed that around 20 percent of the forty-five hundred women who got abortions there came from out of state.[6] And with a number of states now banning abortion after the twentieth week of pregnancy, many women face legal barriers to abortion when second trimester tests reveal a severe fetal anomaly. In such cases, women often travel to states like California or Colorado, where the law permits abortions, on limited grounds, through the twenty-eighth or even thirtieth week of pregnancy.[7]

If abortion remains legal in even one state, it will be available to any woman who can get to that state. This guarantee is built into the structure of our federal system, through the Constitution's Privileges and Immunities Clause, which forbids a state from treating citizens of other states in a discriminatory manner.

Nor can states readily stop their own residents from leaving home in order to get an abortion. The Constitution guarantees the right to travel freely between the states; a state cannot stop a woman from leaving home, even if it knows she's intending to evade its laws.[8]

In effect, if abortion becomes a crime, there will be two laws: one for those who can afford to travel and one for those who cannot. No one believes that women will stop having abortions, simply because they are illegal.

A BLACK-MARKET ABORTION'S PREDICTABLE CONSEQUENCES

Abortion rights sympathizers use the symbol of the coat hanger to call to mind the thousands of women who died from illegal abortions in the years before *Roe v. Wade*. In the decades leading up to the legalization of abortion, an estimated five thousand American women died that way, every year. Make abortion a crime, and the assumption is that we will once again see hospitals filled with women dying from illegal abortions.

A different story emerges when one takes a close look at the mortality rates in countries worldwide today in which abortion is either banned or permitted only to save the mother's life. Consider Latin America, where the vast majority of countries have restrictive laws against abortion. There are approximately 4.6 million illegal abortions in Latin America every year. In 1990, researchers estimated an abortion mortality rate of 30 deaths per 100,000 live births. By 2008, the rate had dropped to 10.

Think of it this way. In 1972, the United States experienced 5,000 abortion-related deaths in a population of 200 million. Today, there are 600 million people in Latin America. At 1972 rates, we'd expect to see 15,000 women dying from illegal abortions every year. Instead, in 2016, there were around 900 deaths.

I want to be clear: the risks of dying from illegal abortion haven't dropped everywhere in the world. In Africa, abortion-related deaths remain high; it's the cause of at least 9 percent of all maternal deaths. As many as 16,000 African women die from illegal abortions every year.[9] But in the world's more industrialized nations, the rate of deaths from illegal abortions has dramatically declined.

Why the difference? Experts point to widespread access to abortion drugs throughout Latin America (and indeed, throughout much of the world, with the exception of Africa). For example, consider the case of Brazil. Exact figures are impossible to determine, as is always the case where abortion is illegal, but experts believe that somewhere between 500,000 and 1 million pregnancies are terminated in Brazil each year. Around half of them are induced using abortion drugs and the rest are performed in clandestine clinics. Between 2003 and 2009, as abortion drugs became easier and easier to procure, the number of women hospitalized from complications from illegal abortions fell by 40,000.[10]

For any woman with a smartphone and money, illegal abortion today is far less risky than it was in 1972. That is to say, the risks of illegal abortion vary by class, age, education level, geographic location, and race.

As a result, we already know what illegal abortions will look like in the United States, in the event that abortion becomes illegal. Remember what we saw in El Salvador: women who live in cities and are educated enough to determine how long they've been pregnant and how to procure the right dose of Cytotec that can end their pregnancies without detection. The medical risks—uncontrolled bleeding and infection from an incomplete abortion—are readily treated. With 25 percent of all pregnancies ending in miscarriage, losing a pregnancy is so commonplace that, in the vast majority of cases, doctors will have no way of knowing whether a woman deliberately ended her pregnancy.

But the risks of illegal abortion vary. A wealthy woman can readily identify and buy unadulterated drugs or access to a well-trained physician. A poor woman will struggle to find accurate information and safe abortion providers. A pregnant teenager living in a Salvadoran village might have a smartphone; almost everyone there does. But chances are that she'll have a harder time safely ending her unwanted pregnancy because she'll be poorer, less educated, and farther away from the cities where she might buy abortion drugs. Even if she finds money to pay for the bus and the abortion drugs, she's less likely than her more educated peers to know how far along her pregnancy is, or how to navigate the black market to find a safe abortion provider.

But we need not look to El Salvador to imagine how the black market in illegal abortion will work here. The United States already is experiencing an increase in illegal abortions. As we saw in chapter 4, with the growing number of regulations governing abortion providers, the costs of accessing abortion have increased. One consequence of increasing the time and money required to get a legal abortion is a rise in the number of women attempting to terminate their pregnancies on their own. A 2015 study by Dr. Dan Grossman confirmed this trend. He surveyed Texas women having clinic-based abortions and found that 7 percent of them had first tried one or more times to terminate their pregnancies on their own.[11]

Hospitals, too, are seeing signs of this trend. For example, in 2015, a Tennessee woman named Anna Yocca attempted to give herself an abortion with a coat hanger in a bath tub. She was twenty-four weeks pregnant. Worried about the excessive bleeding she immediately experienced, Yocca went to the emergency room. She later was charged with attempted murder. A few years earlier, a Tennessee woman's attempt to induce an abortion with a coat hanger led to a life-threatening infection, forcing doctors to perform a hysterectomy.[12] Three recent cases involve women accused of having shot themselves in the belly in an effort to end their pregnancies.[13]

If women already are opting to attempt to end their pregnancies on their own, surely they will continue to do so in greater numbers if abortion becomes illegal and thus even harder to access. And as greater numbers of women attempt to self-abort, we will see an increase in the number of women seeking emergency care after self-abortion.

We already know, having seen what happened in El Salvador, that any effort to enforce laws against abortion will focus on what happens in the emergency room. It is at the emergency room bedside that we can begin to consider the answers to the questions of when and how abortion crimes will be enforced.

THE QUESTION OF ENFORCEMENT

If abortion is a crime, who is the criminal? Will we punish the woman who has an abortion or her doctor? What if there is no doctor involved? How much of our criminal justice resources are we willing to spend on enforcing abortion laws?

The question of how and when abortion will be prosecuted is one of the most intensely disputed issues in our contemporary abortion debate. Abortion rights advocates often assume that, if abortion becomes illegal, women will be targeted. Their position is bolstered by occasional pro-lifers' assertions that "there would have to be some sort of punishment for women," as President Donald Trump said while on the campaign trail in 2016.[14]

But most antiabortion advocates reject this position, explaining that, even if abortion is illegal, women will not be targeted. Rather than seeing women who have illegal abortions as criminals, they see them as abortion's "second victims."[15]

Instead of punishing women, pro-life movement leaders assert that when abortion becomes a crime, abortion doctors, not women, will be punished.[16] Indeed, the official pro-life position labels the suggestion that women could be prosecuted for illegal abortions "pro-choice propaganda." Clarke Forsythe, general counsel of the pro-life advocacy group, Americans United for Life, is emphatic on the subject: "Pro-life legislators and pro-life leaders do not support the prosecution of women and will not push for such a policy when Roe is overturned."[17]

The truth is that both sides are right. As we'll see, abortion laws historically and today typically are not enforced against women but, rather, against those who provide illegal abortions. Nonetheless, in recent years, hundreds of US women have been prosecuted for crimes stemming from their own attempts to terminate their pregnancies.

Prosecuting Abortion

I was surprised to learn how rarely abortion laws are enforced in places where it is illegal. Indeed, it was my desire to understand the scarcity of prosecutions in Chile—despite the ban, there are only a handful of prosecutions a year, mostly against doctors—that inspired this book. Throughout history, and around the world today, abortion-related prosecutions are few and far between.

Professor Leslie Reagan has written a comprehensive history of how the United States enforced its laws against abortion in the years before 1973. In it, she documents a pattern of occasional, local efforts at cracking down on illegal abortion, accompanied by a general tendency to look the other way.[18] And although law enforcement strategies varied over time, the targets for prosecution were almost never women. Instead, the so-called "abortionists" were charged with the crime.[19] However, unless a woman died, these doctors seldom were arrested and even more seldom convicted.[20]

It wasn't that prosecutors could not have charged women with illegal abortion. Most state laws were general, making it illegal for anyone to bring about an abortion. In fifteen states, laws explicitly penalized women who solicited or submitted to an abortion.[21] Some states even made it clear they wanted to target women, enacting laws against "self-abortion." For example, an 1869 New York law criminalized a woman's participation in her own abortion.[22] Even today, there are no fewer than four states with laws on the books that forbid "self-abortion."[23]

Despite the fact that prosecutors could have prosecuted women for having illegal abortions, though, there is no evidence that they did so. In the century or so when abortion was illegal, US historians have found only two cases involving women charged with abortion-related crimes—one in 1911 and another in 1922.[24]

The same pattern prevails throughout the world today in countries where abortion is illegal. Abortion prosecutions are rare. One finds occasional crackdowns, rather than consistent enforcement. There was one in 2007, in Mato Grosso do Sul, a remote state in Brazil, in which officials subpoenaed ten thousand medical records from two decades of practice at a notorious abortion clinic and sentenced three hundred women to perform community service for having committed the crime of abortion.[25] Between 2009 and 2011, several conservative states in Mexico intensified abortion prosecutions, seemingly in response to Mexico City's decision to legalize abortion.[26] Typically, these spikes in prosecution are local, rather than part of a national or even a regional policy or plan. For the most part, prosecutions focus on abortion providers, rather than on the women who seek them.

El Salvador is the exception among countries because it has enforced its abortion laws primarily against women, rather than against their doctors. That's what led me to go there. Law enforcement agents have toured the country's hospitals, urging doctors to report women they suspect of having deliberately ended their pregnancies. Even so, prosecutions are rare. There are, on average, only twelve abortion-related prosecutions a year.[27] And as we saw in chapter 2, most of those cases wind up involving women whose babies die during childbirth. They are not really abortion cases at all.

When abortion is a crime, women are seldom prosecuted. But seldom is not the same as never. A close look at the cases that do get prosecuted, both in the United States and abroad, reveals a striking pattern: they are cases in which there is no doctor to blame.

Which Women Are Prosecuted?

Pro-life advocates explain the decision not to prosecute women by positing that the woman who commits an abortion on herself is not the perpetrator, but the "second victim" of the crime. As notions go, it is not a particularly compelling one.

The claim that women are victimized by abortion might be borne out in a narrow set of cases. A woman looking for love puts her trust in a bad man who leaves her pregnant and alone. One can see this narrative at work in the following excerpt, from pro-life Amherst College jurisprudence professor Hadley Arkes:

> On the one hand there may be a young, unmarried woman, who finds herself pregnant, with the father of the child not standing with her. Abandoned by the man, and detached from her family, she may feel the burden of the crisis bearing on her alone, with the prospect of life-altering changes.[28]

The problem with the "second victim" exception to abortion prosecutions is that not all women fit the pattern. Not all women who have abortions look like victims, or at least not like the sort of victims Arkes might recognize.

Life typically is more complicated than a morality play, after all. Sometimes there are many men or no man in particular. Sometimes the woman is on drugs. Sometimes she ends her pregnancy on her own; there is no doctor to blame. Unsurprisingly, as the narrative shifts, so too does the extent to which the woman is perceived as a second victim of abortion.

So long as there is a doctor or a faithless lover in the picture, it is possible to understand the crime of illegal abortion as having two victims, with the doctor or the absconding lover emerging as the only criminal. What happens, though, when there is no third party involved?

In recent decades, law enforcement officials have charged hundreds of US women with crimes relating to pregnancy or abortion. This is true even though abortion is legal. Pro-choice advocates see these prosecutions as evidence that it will become routine for states to charge women with abortion crimes if abortion becomes illegal. Pro-life advocates object, insisting that these prosecutions involve extraordinary facts—not simple illegal abortions—and therefore the women involved merit punishment.

The dispute is complicated because the cases aren't necessarily straightforward. Regardless, one fact unites almost all the prosecutions to date: these are cases in which there are no doctors to blame for the harm done to the fetus. And it turns out that, without a third party to blame, the law sees the women not as second victims but, rather, as criminals.

A 2013 article offered the first systematic investigation into cases in which officials have endeavored to restrict and punish pregnant women for harming their fetuses. Authors Lynn Paltrow and Jeanne Flavin identified and analyzed 413 cases from 1973 to 2005.[29] Drawing their data from a thorough review of newspaper articles and court dockets, and including only cases that were fully adjudicated by the time of publication, their study offers an overview of the range of ways in which the legal system has targeted pregnant women.

Some of the cases they found seem unrelated to abortion, such as those targeting women accused of using drugs or alcohol while pregnant. Indeed, most of the interventions they identified concerned women who sought not to terminate, but rather to continue their pregnancies. The women in these cases typically were restrained, and even prosecuted, for behaving in ways that risked harming their fetuses. But many of the cases Paltrow and Flavin identified did involve women who were prosecuted for illegally ending their pregnancies. The truth is that, around the country today, women are being prosecuted for having illegal abortions.

You might wonder how a woman can be prosecuted for illegal abortion, if abortion is legal in the United States? The answer lies in the fact that we regulate abortion, as we do all health procedures. Abortion is only legal when it is performed in compliance with these regulations. At the very least, this means that to be legal, an abortion must be performed by a licensed doctor. Therefore, a woman who ends her pregnancy on her own can be understood to have had an illegal abortion.

Paltrow, a lawyer who has for decades been defending women accused of illegal abortion and other pregnancy-related crimes, notes that, between 1973 and 2013, at least 413 women were prosecuted for illegal abortions.[30] These cases range from alleged illegal abortions to claims arising out of miscarriages, stillbirths, or perceived risks taken while pregnant and thought to have contributed to the death of the fetus.[31] Women have been prosecuted in cases of fetal demise in nineteen different states, and not only for illegal abortion, but for a variety of related crimes as well.[32]

The prosecutions stand in stark contradiction to the claim that women will not be punished for abortion because they are "abortion's second victims." The common thread in these cases is that they almost always involve women who acted on their own, rather than with the help of an abortion provider. With no one else to be the "perpetrator," a prosecutor might see the woman not as a victim, but instead as a criminal.

The facts underlying many of these prosecutions testify to the ways in which abortion regulations already restrict abortion access, leading desperate women to attempt unsafe abortions. If these sorts of self-abortion cases are arising while abortion is still legal, then we are sure to see more of them if and when abortion becomes illegal. As such, it's helpful to examine one such prosecution in detail, so we can better understand how the law can be invoked to punish a woman suspected of having illegally terminated her pregnancy.

———

In July 2013, Purvi Patel was charged with two crimes relating to the death of her fetus. A disclosure here: I followed the case closely not only because it interested me, but also because my spouse was her appellate defense lawyer.

Patel was unmarried and living with her parents, who were devout Hindu immigrants, when she became pregnant. She worried about how her parents would respond to her violation of their norms surrounding premarital sex and out-of-wedlock pregnancy. These concerns were intensified by the fact that she had been having an affair with a married coworker.

Estimating that she was at most three months' pregnant, Patel determined to end the pregnancy without her parents' knowledge. After learning that a trip to the nearest abortion clinic would take over three hours and that she would need to return twice in order to have the procedure, Patel found an online advertisement for abortion pills, sold by an overseas pharmacy. She ordered the drugs, and when they arrived two weeks later, she took them.

It turned out that her pregnancy was far more advanced than she'd thought. After ingesting the pills, Patel delivered a one-and-a-half-pound baby of approximately twenty-five to twenty-six weeks' gestation in the bathroom of the home she shared with her parents.

She arrived at the emergency room, hemorrhaging and having lost 20 percent of her total blood volume. After several hours of emergency surgery, she awoke surrounded by police officials, who questioned her about the whereabouts of her missing fetus. When authorities located the body, the state of Indiana charged Patel with both felony child neglect and feticide. After trial, she was sentenced to twenty years in prison.

There is a stark contrast in the ways in which the pro-choice and pro-life media responded to Patel's conviction. The pro-choice world was outraged by Patel's prosecution, asserting that she was innocent, and that she had been sentenced for having a miscarriage.[33] By contrast, the pro-life world saw Patel as a monster:

> [W]hat happened here wasn't just an abortion. . . . Granted, the line between legal abortion and criminal feticide isn't a bright one. Both kill a child whose existence is disagreeable to someone. But someone who seeks out an abortionist at least has the excuse that a professional the law says she can trust lied to her and withheld key information about what abortion really was.[34]

Those who supported Patel's conviction worried that pro-choice advocates would use the case "as a golden opportunity to push the meme that pro-lifers are secretly clamoring to throw post-abortive women in jail."[35] They insisted that the facts were otherwise, pointing to the fetus's gestational age and the illegal drugs as distinguishing factors.[36]

On appeal, the Indiana appellate court overturned Patel's conviction for feticide, finding that feticide laws did not apply to pregnant women, but only to third parties. However, the court upheld her conviction on the lesser charge of neglect of a child.[37]

The debate over Patel's case has much to teach us about how women might come to be prosecuted if abortion becomes a crime. Prosecutions will be reserved for exceptional cases—those in which the woman does not seem like a second victim to the prosecutor. And the most important factor in determining whether a woman will be seen as abortion's second victim is whether there is someone else to view as the perpetrator.

Consider how we might have responded to Patel if, rather than taking illegal abortion drugs, she had been given an abortion by her best friend Fay, a medical technician who had advised Patel about buying the drugs. If Fay had performed an abortion on Patel, I suspect the law would have viewed Fay, rather than Patel, as the perpetrator. How could she have preyed upon her trusting, vulnerable friend? How did she overlook the possibility that Patel's pregnancy was too far along? She jeopardized Patel's life.

With Fay cast as the perpetrator, it would have been possible to see Patel as a second victim, as an innocent woman whose life was endangered at the hands of the real monster. If there is a moral justification for punishing a woman who induces her own abortion, but not one who hires another to do so for her, it is not clear to me.

The second and more important lesson we learn from Patel's case is that individual actors, rather than official policies, determine whether and how the law is enforced. The decision to report Patel to the police, the decision to prosecute her for a homicide offense—these were judgment calls made by individual doctors and prosecutors.

Paltrow and Flavin's forty-year study of pregnancy crimes demonstrates that Patel's case was not unique in this regard. Instead, these cases demonstrate a dramatic pattern of selective law enforcement. Although women have been charged with pregnancy-related crimes in forty-four states and the District of Columbia, more than 50 percent of these prosecutions were in the South. One state, South Carolina, accounts for 93 of the 413 cases.[38] Further analysis shows that "in individual states, cases tend to cluster in particular counties and sometimes in particular hospitals":

[I]n South Carolina thirty-four of the ninety-three cases came from the contiguous counties of Charleston and Berkeley. Staff at one hospital, the Medical University of South Carolina, initiated thirty of these cases. In Florida twenty-five of the fifty-five cases took place in Escambia County. Of these, twenty-three came from just two hospitals: Sacred Heart Hospital and Baptist Hospital. In Missouri twenty-six of the twenty-nine cases came from Jackson County. Of these, twenty cases came from a single hospital: Truman Medical Center.[39]

This pattern of prosecution—one hospital, one county—speaks to individual crusaders, rather than careful policy making. And the resulting cases expose the most profound problem with this individualized exercise of legal power: it is unmistakably biased against the most marginalized women in society.

Paltrow and Flavin found that almost 60 percent of the 413 cases in their study involved poor women of color. Needless to say, this rate far exceeds their representative share of the population.[40] In spite of overwhelming evidence demonstrating that pregnant women of all races and classes abuse drugs at similar rates, 84 percent of these prosecutions were brought against minority women charged with having used an illegal drug.[41]

Where are the white women?

For decades, doctors and prosecutors have used the force of law to sanction poor pregnant women and, particularly, poor women of color.[42] We saw this pattern in El Salvador, where the women prosecuted in relation to abortion are overwhelming poor, uneducated, and rural. And we will see more of it here, among poor minority women, as we intensify abortion restrictions.

If history is any indication of what to expect should abortion become illegal, we will need to append an asterisk to the promise that women won't be punished for abortion. The truth is, wealthy women will not be punished.

Poor women may be prosecuted, though—particularly minority women who seek care at public hospitals after attempting to end their own pregnancies. There won't be many such prosecutions; most doctors will opt to maintain their patients' confidentiality.

But we can be sure we will see some cases growing out of this scenario. We already have.

CONCLUSION

We started this chapter by recognizing the underlying questions one must ask about making abortion a crime: Will it stop abortions? If not, who will the law target, and who is it likely to catch?

We've seen the answers to these questions, hiding in plain view: abortion will remain legal in some states and, where it is not, illegal abortion will be prevalent.

We've seen enough to know that abortion prosecutions will be rare, and they will be set in motion not by an overarching policy but, rather, according to the moral sensibilities of individual actors. We've seen how these individual actors will tend to target the most marginalized women in society.

I haven't yet mentioned the indirect consequences of banning abortion. There is more that we can predict will happen as a consequence of making abortion a crime. First, we're likely to see a rise in births to teenagers. Compared to adults, teenagers are less likely to use contraception, and they are slower to recognize that they are pregnant. Once they are pregnant, teenagers have a hard time accessing illegal abortions. In addition to being younger, less educated, and more vulnerable in general, teens typically lack the money and the mobility necessary to get abortions on their own.

In El Salvador, the consequences of the abortion ban fall disproportionately on teenage girls. The country has one of the highest teen pregnancy rates in Latin America. Even as teen pregnancy rates are dropping in the United States and elsewhere worldwide, El Salvador's rates are rising. A 2014 National Family Health Survey report notes that 23 percent of Salvadoran women ages fifteen to nineteen have had a child before age eighteen.[43] There are serious long-term costs associated with teen motherhood, for the mother and child, and for society at large. Teen mothers are disproportionately likely to drop out of school. They are more likely than older mothers to raise their families in poverty, with negative consequences for the entire family's health, education, and long-term stability.

Nor is teen motherhood the only consequence of the abortion ban for adolescent girls. In addition, where abortion is illegal, one finds elevated rates of suicide among pregnant teens.[44] In El Salvador, hundreds of pregnant girls commit suicide every year.[45] Indeed, suicide is the highest cause of death among the country's pregnant girls.

There is every reason to believe we will see similar patterns among US teens in places where abortion becomes illegal. Although we are a wealthier country, the factors driving El Salvador's teens to pregnancy, motherhood, and even suicide would be the same here. Here, too, teenagers will struggle to identify options when faced with an unplanned pregnancy. Here, too, teens are prone to catastrophic thinking. We can predict with certainty the news stories we're likely to read, in places where abortion is illegal: rates of births to teens will rise, and on occasion, some of our poorest, most isolated pregnant teens will feel there is no way out but death.

So, what are we to make of these facts? How are we to weigh the significance of what we know will and won't happen, if *Roe* falls and states can make abortion a crime?

It is important to remember Beatriz's case in considering our answers. Those who morally oppose abortion derive an intangible, yet vitally important benefit from a law that reinforces their view. The law plays a significant role in helping to express collective values—to set as ideals, if not as norms, the things we hold to be true.

We saw the lengths to which El Salvador was willing to go in order to defend the principles embodied in its abortion ban. By permitting Beatriz to end her pregnancy, but only in self-defense—only when the threat of her death became imminent—El Salvador stayed true to its position that a fetus has the same rights as any other human being.

For many, many Americans, the idea that the law makes abortion legal, without qualification, is anathema. They will not rest easily until the law is aligned with their moral position.

In addition to resting more easily, abortion opponents believe that banning abortion may also have some deterrent effect on abortion rates. As we've seen, there's no evidence in the aggregate to support the claim that banning abortion reduces abortion rates. Indeed, we've seen that abortion rates are actually higher in countries where it is illegal than in countries where abortion is legal. Still, it stands to reason that, by banning abortion, some women who otherwise would have aborted will carry their pregnancies to term. We just don't know how many.

Which brings us back to Cass Sunstein's admonition against fanaticism: The true test of a law's validity lies in assessing not simply its message but also its impact.[46]

Is it worth it to you?

I can't answer that question. But I am absolutely certain that you need to do so. It's at the center of the only meaningful conversation to be had about abortion laws.

PARTING THOUGHTS ON LEAVING BEHIND THE ABORTION WAR

As I put this journey behind me, I'm struck by my feelings of nostalgia. I'll miss the conversations. I'll miss hearing the stories.

For it's clear that's what I've been doing all along. Collecting stories. The stories people told me about how they thought about abortion and abortion laws felt surprisingly private. They were personal, like secrets.

Our abortion battle is so constrained by slogans that we almost never get to talk about the ideas that underlie our positions, the things that lead us to care about the abortion issue in the first place. By this, I mean the big questions: what we make of sex, motherhood, love, the purpose and meaning of life.

I will miss the way, time and again, strangers moved me to tears. How I sat in the gigantic gun store with Oklahoma senator Mike Reynolds and heard him speak of his faith that life begins at the moment of conception. How I cried when he described the guilt and the pain he felt about his wife's use of contraception that prevented implantation, causing the fertilized eggs to pass, month after month. He didn't persuade me to change, or even to reconsider, my position on legalized abortion. But he helped me see the world, for a time, through his eyes.

You see, before this journey, it's not just that I didn't understand how pro-life advocates thought about abortion laws. It's also that I had come to view pro-lifers in broad generalities, as if they were two-dimensional objects, not subjects.

And unlike subjects, it's easy to dismiss objects with contempt.

I'm reminded of a favorite passage from George Orwell's Spanish Civil War memoir, *Homage to Catalonia*, in which he recalls catching sight of a Fascist soldier on a dawn reconnaissance mission. The man was holding up his pants as he ran, and Orwell couldn't bring himself to shoot him. "I had come to Spain to shoot Fascists," he said, "but a man who is holding up his trousers isn't a 'Fascist,' he is visibly a fellow creature."[1]

The most painful moment in my journey still stings, years later: it was when I learned how Tony Lauinger had characterized me. "She is pro-abortion," he'd said. "Long experience has taught me that there's nothing to be gained by helping gather intelligence from behind enemy lines from seemingly well-meaning academics."

Everything Lauinger said about me is pretty much true, although I bristle at the label "pro-abortion." I'm an academic, I'm pro-choice, and I suppose that this project, like all of my work, might therefore be seen as coming from behind enemy lines.

So it is puzzling, at first, to understand why his words made me feel as if he'd kicked the breath out of me. It's because he'd rendered me two-dimensional. I can't recognize myself in his description of me. He'd reduced me to a set of categories, to an object that he could regard with distrust and contempt.

We pay a moral price for dehumanizing other human beings. Contempt and distrust corrode our ability to connect. They prevent us from recognizing ourselves in one another. They keep us apart.

We pay a practical price, too. Our mutual contempt leaves us locked in debate over the question of whether abortion should be legal. And as we've seen, that question is not serving us well. It's distracting us from the better question of how we think things will change if abortion is illegal.

That's the question I would have liked to ask Lauinger.

To be sure, abortion laws have symbolic importance. Both sides in the abortion war care deeply about the messages sent by laws governing abortion. The pro-life world's outrage that abortion legalizes killing is matched by the pro-choice world's insistence upon the full legal autonomy of women. Honestly, I don't see how we'll ever resolve our ideological differences.

In the meantime, though, our blinkered focus on whether abortion should be legal distracts us from the plight of the women and children most affected by our abortion laws. You met them in chapter 4 during journeys through Oklahoma and California: they are the most marginalized women in the country. Another child will thrust them deeper into poverty, but an abortion does little to lift them out of it. The war over abortion law draws our gaze away from them, relieving us of the obligation to notice, if not to reset, the odds against them.

I think back on former Oklahoma House speaker Steele's comment that "the best way to lower abortion rates is to deal with what causes women to want to abort in the first place." It was a wistful observation, an afterthought to our conversation, yet it was also a point of complete agreement between us—a blue-state, pro-choice feminist and a red-state, pro-life minister.

What would it look like to design a policy around the idea that no one should have to choose abortion because she is too poor to have a child? It would cost billions of dollars. Yet, we routinely spend such sums on the war over abortion's legality. Might it be worth it to try something different?

I dedicated this book to the women at Birth Choice of Oklahoma, and to those at Access Women's Health Justice because they share core values that transcend our endless war over abortion. Both organizations understand how the deck is stacked against poor women and their children.

I have a fantasy that, if I could just get them in the same room, talking about their clients, they'd see one another as kindred spirits. Maybe they'd forge an alliance. The battle over abortion law would rage in the distance, but in the living room, plans would be made to launch a new way of harnessing our power for the good.

The hardest thing would be learning to listen to one another, for deep listening is the prerequisite to any meaningful conversation. It will take extraordinary patience to look past the trappings of our abortion team allegiances. But we don't need to abandon our respective teams to sit together and recognize our shared goals.

And in that hard-won conversation, we would not take long to realize that this fight over abortion laws is not the only battle women face. It's not even the most important one.

ACKNOWLEDGMENTS

My deepest thanks to those who have helped me along the way. To my editors at Beacon Press: Alexis Rizzuto, who saw the potential, and Rachael Marks, who brought it home, helping me hear my own voice and knowing precisely when to praise effusively and when to pause. Thanks also to the production team for continual and kind support.

To Santa Clara University and its Jesuit mission, which provided for all my needs: time, money, students, and intellectual freedom.

To Peter Handler and Ariella Radwin, more midwives than readers. You coaxed my stories out of me, comforting me when the telling grew hard, listening so closely you understood what I wanted to say long before I figured out how to say it.

To all those I met on my journey. Thank you for trusting a stranger with your stories. It was a gift to sit in intimate, earnest conversation. So different from the distorted rhetoric with which we fight our abortion war. Whether or not you're mentioned, every conversation I had helped shape my understanding of the stories I've told herein. Your vision helped clarify my own. I carry you with me, and am grateful for the company.

To those in El Salvador, heroic in the face of struggles larger than any I've known. In particular, to the Agrupación Ciudadana por la Despenalizacion del Aborto, without whom I never would have taken this journey. To Hermana Peggy O'Neill and Centro Arte Para la Paz, for sheltering my body and feeding my soul. To the lay midwives of

Suchitoto, "Las Estrellas," Angeles, Darlyn, Johanna, Vilma, Zulema, and Yanira, for being my teachers.

To the folks at Oklahoma City University Law School, who opened doors and minds, most notably my own. In particular, I am indebted to Lawrence Hellman, Arthur LeFrancois, Andrew Spiropoulos, and Dr. Eli Reshef.

To Trisha Cobb, for deep insight and superb research assistance.

Thanks also to those who read drafts: Felice Batlan, Khiara Bridges, Suzanne Carey, Paula Dempsey, Father Paul Goda, Ed Goldman, Liz Klein, Art LeFrancois, Rachel Marshall, Lynn Morgan, Hanna Oberman, Sarah Roberts, Carole Joffe, and Andrew Spiropoulos. And to those who helped workshop my ideas: Tracy Weitz, Carole Joffe, and the Bixby Center for Global Reproductive Health, my colleagues at Santa Clara University Law, my students in Abortion & the Law (spring 2015), Chicago-Kent College of Law faculty workshop, American Bar Foundation workshop, and 2017 anthropology students and faculty at Mt. Holyoke College and Smith College.

Finally, to my friends and family. To Kathy Baker, Dina Kaplan, and Sarah Delson, for helping me shout down my demons. And to Larry Marshall, Rachel Marshall, Shlomie Marshall, Jaclyn Marshall, Yoni Marshall, Liz Klien, Hanna Obermen, and Noa Oberman, for letting me make abortion "table talk." I am so very blessed by your presence in my life.

So many have helped, in so many ways, over the years I've worked on this project that I'm sure I've forgotten some names. These omissions belong alongside the other mistakes I'm sure to have made in these pages. Unintentional, and mine alone.

NOTES

Introduction

1. David Foster Wallace, *This Is Water: Some Thoughts, Delivered on a Significant Occasion, About Living a Compassionate Life* (Boston: Little, Brown and Company, 2009).
2. Michelle Oberman, "Sex, Drugs, Pregnancy, and the Law: Rethinking the Problems of Pregnant Women Who Use Drugs," *Hastings Law Journal* 43 (1991–92): 505, http://digitalcommons.law.scu.edu/facpubs/518/.
3. M. Schäfer, B. Schnack, and M. Soyka, "Sexual and Physical Abuse During Early Childhood or Adolescence and Later Drug Addiction," *Psychotherapie Psychosomatik Medizinische Psychologie* (2000), http://www.ncbi.nlm.nih.gov/pubmed/10721277.
4. Michelle Oberman, "Eva and Her Baby (a Story of Adolescent Sex, Pregnancy, Longing, Love, Loneliness, and Death)," *Duke Journal of Gender Law & Policy* 16 (2009): 213–22, http://digitalcommons.law.scu.edu/facpubs/44/.
5. Indeed, it has become common for states to enact ten or more such laws in a single legislative session. Steven Ertlet, "States Pass More Pro-Life Laws Saving Babies from Abortions in Last 5 Years Than the Previous 15," LifeNews.com, January 4, 2016, www.lifenews.com/2016/01/04/states-pass-more-pro-life-laws-saving-babies-from-abortions-in-last-5-fives-than-the-previous-15/. These new laws govern practices ranging from prohibitions on buying human eggs to mandating physician disclosure of misleading and often inaccurate information. Texas and Arizona have passed laws requiring doctors to tell patients that the abortion drugs they are about to take can be reversed, should they change their minds and decide to keep their pregnancy. This in spite of the lack of any medical evidence proving it is true. Rick Rojas, "Arizona Orders Doctors to Say Abortions with Drugs May Be Reversible," *New York Times*,

March 31, 2015, http://www.nytimes.com/2015/04/01/us/politics/arizona
-doctors-must-say-that-abortions-with-drugs-may-be-reversed.html. Other
states require doctors to tell patients that abortion is correlated with
elevated risks of breast cancer and suicide—findings lacking scientific
support and rejected by the relevant medical authorities. Guttmacher Institute, "Counseling and Waiting Periods for Abortion," *State Policies in
Brief (as of June 2013)*, http://www.guttmacher.org/statecenter/spibs/spib
_MWPA.pdf.

6. For a detailed recounting of her story, see Michelle Oberman, "Judging
Vanessa: Norm Setting and Deviance in the Law of Motherhood," *Wil-
liam and Mary Journal of Women and the Law* 15 (2009): 337–59, http://
digitalcommons.law.scu.edu/facpubs/498/.

7. Estimates range from sixty thousand to three hundred thousand abortions
annually. E. Prada and H. Ball, "Induced Abortion in Chile," In Brief,
Guttmacher Institute, 2016, https://www.guttmacher.org/sites/default/files
/pdfs/pubs/journals/IB_Abortion-Chile.pdf.

8. In the United States, legal induced abortion results in only 0.6 deaths per
100,000 procedures. Worldwide, unsafe abortion accounts for a death
rate that is 350 times higher (220 per 100,000), and, in Sub-Saharan Africa, the rate is 800 times higher, at 460 per 100,000. "Facts on Induced
Abortion Worldwide," In Brief, Guttmacher Institute, 2012, http://www
.who.int/reproductivehealth/publications/unsafe_abortion/induced
_abortion_2012.pdf. See also Department of Reproductive Health and
Research, World Health Organization, *Unsafe Abortion: Global and
Regional Estimates of the Incidence of Unsafe Abortion and Associated
Mortality in 2008*, sixth ed. (Geneva: World Health Organization, 2011),
http://www.who.int/reproductivehealth/publications/unsafe_abortion
/9789241501118/en/.

9. E. Koch, "Impact of Reproductive Laws on Maternal Mortality: The
Chilean Natural Experiment," *Linacre Quarterly* (2013), http://www
.melisainstitute.org/uploads/1/2/3/9/12398427/koch_2014_rev_chil
_obstet_79_5_351_en2.pdf.

10. Lidia Casas Becerra, "Women Prosecuted and Imprisoned for Abortion
in Chile," *Reproductive Health Matters* (1997), http://www.rhm-elsevier
.com/article/S0968–8080(97)90003–3/pdf. See also Lidia Casas and
Lieta Vivaldi, "Abortion in Chile: The Practice Under a Restrictive Re-
gime," *Reproductive Health Matters* (2014), http://www.academia
.edu/10146213/Abortion_in_Chile_the_practice_under_a_restrictive
_regime.

Chapter 1: Beatriz and Her Case

1. Guillermo Ortiz, perinatologist at La Maternidad Hospital, in discussion with the author, June 2014 (notes on file with author).
2. Penal Code of El Salvador 1998, Title 1, Crimes Related to Life, Chapter II, Crimes Related to Unborn Humans, Art. 133–139, http://www.oas.org/dil/esp/Codigo_Penal_El_Salvador.pdf; Soledad Varela, "Persecuted: Political Process and Abortion Legislation in El Salvador: A Human Rights Analysis," *Center for Reproductive Law & Policy* 27 (2001): 96n130, http://reproductiverights.org/sites/default/files/documents/persecuted1.pdf, http://www.reproductiverights.org/sites/default/files/documents/persecuted2.pdf; "El Salvador," in UN Population Division Department of Economic and Social Affairs, *Abortion Policies: A Global Review* (June 2002), http://www.un.org/esa/population/publications/abortion/profiles.htm.
3. Guillermo Ortiz, author interview.
4. "Ectopic Pregnancy," Cedars-Sinai, https://www.cedars-sinai.edu/Patients/Health-Conditions/Ectopic-Pregnancy.aspx, accessed November 8, 2016.
5. Alejandro Guidos, MD, president of El Salvador's Association of Obstetricians and Gynecologists, in discussion with the author, June 2014.
6. Oswaldo Ernesto Feusier, "Pasado Y Presente Del Delito De Aborto En El Salvador," *Universidad Centroamericana "Jose Simeon Cañas"* (2016), 135n, http://www.uca.edu.sv/deptos/ccjj/media/archivo/95bbb4_pasadoy presentedeldelitodeabortoenelsalvador.pdf.
7. Loida Martínez and Suchit Chavez, "Salud aboga por aborto terapéutico a mujer enferma," *La Prensa Grafica*, April 17, 2013, http://www.laprensagrafica.com/Salud-aboga-por-aborto-terapeutico-a-mujer-enferma.
8. "Red Familia rechaza aborto de Beatriz," editorial, *La Pagina*, April 18, 2013, http://www.lapagina.com.sv/nacionales/80505/2013/04/19/Red-Familia-rechaza-aborto-de-Beatriz.
9. Carmen Rodriguez, "Mamá de Beatriz: 'No quiero que mi hija muera,'" *La Pagina*, May 14, 2013, http://www.lapagina.com.sv/nacionales/81629/2013/05/15/Mama-de-Beatriz-No-quiero-que-mi-hija-muera.
10. Although there is no information about El Salvador's IML online, see this description of Colombia's IML: Medicina Legal y Ciencias Forenses, http://www.medicinalegal.gov.co/en/quienes-somos;jsessionid=2BB1C1 A65FC88B98BAA84D741EA0CC34, accessed May 31, 2017.
11. Jose Miguel Fortin Magana, MD, director of the Instituto de Medicina Legal, in discussion with the author, June 2014.
12. "El Salvador," Center for Justice & Accountability, http://cja.org/where-we-work/el-salvador/.

13. Pew Research Center, *Religion in Latin America: Widespread Change in a Historically Catholic Region* (Washington, DC: November 13, 2014), http://www.pewforum.org/2014/11/13/religion-in-latin-america/.

14. Paul Glader, "Christianity Is Growing Rapidly in El Salvador," *Washington Post*, April 8, 2015, https://www.washingtonpost.com/news/acts-of -faith/wp/2015/04/08/christianity-is-growing-rapidly-in-el-salvador-along -with-gang-violence-and-murder-rates/.

15. Xochitl Sandoval, MD, gynecologist, in discussion with the author, June 2014.

16. Alejandro Guidos, author interview. Guidos explained his association's opinion as a matter of scientific fact: "It's well known that a pregnant patient with Lupus is considered high risk, especially if she had preeclampsia in a prior pregnancy. So, taking all this into account, and finally because of the fetal abnormality, we published an opinion supporting the termination of pregnancy."

17. Christian Melendez, "La Sala de lo Constitucional recibió ayer el informe médico que había solicitado sobre la joven con lupus," *La Prensa Grafica*, May 8, 2013, http://www.laprensagrafica.com/iml—beatriz-puede -continuar-con-su-embarazo.

18. Fortin Magana, author interview.

19. Carmen Rodriguez, "Salud pone en duda resultados de Medicina Legal en caso de Beatriz," *La Pagina*, May 11, 2016, http://www.lapagina.com.sv /nacionales/81502/2013/05/11/Salud-pone-en-duda-resultados-de -Medicina-Legal-en-caso-de-Beatriz.

20. "El Presidente de El Salvador dice que la mujer que pidió aborto tiene el derecho a decidir," *Qué!*, May 13, 2013, http://www.que.es/ultimas -noticias/espana/201305132346-presidente-salvador-dice-mujer-pidio -efe.html.

21. Maria R. Sahuquillo, "Beatriz: Pido al presidente Funes que salve mi vida," *El Pais*, http://sociedad.elpais.com/sociedad/2013/05/30/actualidad /1369922985_768623.html; Karla Zabludovsky, "A Salvadoran at Risk Tests Abortion Law," *New York Times*, May 28, 2013, http://www .nytimes.com/2013/05/29/world/americas/pregnant-sick-and-pressing -salvadoran-abortion-law.html.

22. Adam Cassandra, "HLI President Calls on El Salvador Supreme Court to Protect Life," *Human Life International News*, May 16, 2013, http:// www.hli.org/2013/05/hli-president-calls-on-el-salvador-supreme-court -to-protect-life/.

23. "En defensa de nuestra soberania" (author's translation), elsalvador.com, May 8, 2013, http://www.elsalvador.com/opinion/editoriales/106401/en -defensa-de-nuestra-soberania/.
24. Amnesty International, *On the Brink of Death: Violence Against Women and the Abortion Ban in El Salvador* (2014), https://www.amnestyusa .org/sites/default/files/el_salvador_report_-_on_the_brink_of_death.pdf.
25. Nelson Rauda Zablah, "Magistrates Finalized 'Historic' Hearing to Resolve Abortion Petition," *La Prensa Grafica*, May 17, 2013, http://www .laprensagrafica.com/csj-da-un-plazo-maximo-de-15-dias-para-caso-beatriz.
26. Karla Aabludovsky and Gene Palumbo, "Salvadoran Court Denies Abortion to Ailing Woman," *New York Times*, May 29, 2013, http://mobile .nytimes.com/2013/05/30/world/americas/salvadoran-court-denies-abortion -to-ailing-woman.html?from=world.
27. Corte Suprema de Justicia, *Case BC*, Amparo 310–2013 at 10 (El Salvador).
28. Guillermo Ortiz, author interview.
29. Thomas Aquinas is credited with introducing the principle of double-effect in his discussion of the permissibility of self-defense in the *Summa Theologica* (II-II, Qu. 64, Art. 7). Killing one's assailant is justified, he argues, provided one does not intend to kill him. "Doctrine of Double Effect," *Stanford Encyclopedia of Philosophy*, revised September 23, 2014, http://plato.stanford.edu/entries/double-effect/, accessed May 31, 2017. See also "The Principle of Double Effect," Catholics United for Faith, November 1997, http://www.cuf.org/FileDownloads/doubleeffect.pdf, accessed May 31, 2017.
30. Jorge Ramirez, MD, chief assistant to the minister of health, in discussion with the author, June 2014.
31. Wayne R. LaFave, *Substantive Criminal Law* § 10.4, at 142, second ed. (St. Paul, MN: Thomson/West, 2003).
32. The fundamental right to life and enjoyment of health appear in the Salvadoran Constitution.
33. Corte Suprema de Justicia, *Case BC*, Amparo 310–2013, at 22 (El Salvador). "In the event of termination of the pregnancy after twenty weeks gestation, the aim is not to destroy the fetus, and that the medical team will take all necessary measures to ensure, as far as possible, extrauterine life."
34. LaFave, *Substantive Criminal Law*.
35. Corte Suprema de Justicia, *Case BC*, Amparo 310–2013, at 14 (El Salvador).

36. Karla Zabludovsky, "A Salvadoran at Risk Tests Abortion Law," *New York Times*, May 28, 2013, http://www.nytimes.com/2013/05/29/world /americas/pregnant-sick-and-pressing-salvadoran-abortion-law.html.
37. A zygote is the fertilized egg cell that results from the union of a female gamete (egg, or ovum) with a male gamete (sperm). In embryonic development, the zygote stage is brief and is followed by cleavage, when the single cell becomes subdivided into smaller cells. The zygote represents the first stage in the development of a genetically unique organism. *Encyclopaedia Britannica Online*, s.v. "zygote," https://www.britannica.com /science/zygote, accessed November 8, 2016.
38. Cass R. Sunstein, "On the Expressive Function of Law," *University of Pennsylvania Law Review* 144 (1996): 2021, 2031.
39. Ibid., 2045.
40. Ibid., 2047.

Chapter 2: Assessing the Impact of El Salvador's Abortion Ban

1. Penal Code of El Salvador 1998, Title 1, Crimes Related to Life, Chapter II, Crimes Related to Unborn Humans, Art. 133–139, http://www.oas.org /dil/esp/Codigo_Penal_El_Salvador.pdf.
2. Abortion being illegal, it is hard to get accurate information about the rates of abortion. The WHO bases its estimations on numbers of women hospitalized for abortion complications (where available) and information on the safety of abortion, as well as on findings from surveys of women and studies using an indirect abortion estimation methodology from countries where those were available. E-mail from Dr. Gilda Sedgh, Guttmacher Institute, to author, July 7, 2012 (on file with author). See article by Gilda Sedgh, https://www.guttmacher.org/sites/default/files/pdfs/pubs /journals/Sedgh-Lancet-2012–01.pdf.
3. A recent survey by the El Salvador Ministry of Health reported 19,290 between 2005 and 2008; other surveys put that number as the annual average. See Nina Strochlic, "On the Front Lines of El Salvador's Underground Abortion Economy," *Foreign Policy*, January 3, 2017, http://foreignpolicy.com/2017/01/03/on-the-front-lines-of-el-salvadors -underground-abortion-economy/?utm_source=Sailthru&utm_medium =email&utm_campaign=New+Campaign&utm_term=%2AEditors +Picks.
4. Vinod Mishra, Victor Gaigbe-Togbe, and Julia Ferre, *Abortion Policies and Reproductive Health Around the World* (New York: UN Department of Economic and Social Affairs, Population Division, 2014), http://www

NOTES 151

.un.org/en/development/desa/population/publications/pdf/policy/Abortion
PoliciesReproductiveHealth.pdf, accessed January 24, 2017.
5. For an excellent history of abortion in pre-*Roe* America, see Leslie J.
Reagan, *When Abortion Was a Crime: Women, Medicine, and Law in
the United States, 1867–1973* (Berkeley: University of California Press,
1996), http://ark.cdlib.org/ark:/13030/ft967nb5z5/. For an equally rich
history of abortion doctors in pre-*Roe* America, see Carole E. Joffe, *Doctors of Conscience: The Struggle to Provide Abortion Before and After
Roe v. Wade* (Boston: Beacon Press, 1995).
6. Tekoa King and Mary Brucker, "Pharmacology for Women's Health,"
Journal of Midwifery & Women's Health 55 (2010): 394, doi:10.1016
/j.jmwh.2010.05.005.
7. Mifeprex, *RxList*, http://www.rxlist.com/mifeprex-ru486-drug.htm,
accessed June 2, 2017.
8. Beverly Winikoff and Wendy Sheldon, "Use of Medicines Changing the
Face of Abortion," *International Perspectives on Sexual and Reproductive Health* 38, no. 3 (September 6, 2012), https://www.guttmacher.org
/about/journals/ipsrh/2012/09/use-medicines-changing-face-abortion.
The most widely available illegal abortion drug in Latin America is misoprostol (brand name is Cytotec), which is less effective than mifepristone
(brand name is Mifeprex). Nguyen Thi Nhu Ngoc et al., "Comparing
Two Early Medical Abortion Regimens: Mifepristone Plus Misoprostol
vs. Misoprostol Alone," *Contraception* 83, no. 5 (2011): 410–17.
9. "Abortion Induction with Misoprostol Alone in Pregnancies Through 9
Weeks' LMP," Gynuity, October 2013, http://gynuity.org/resources/read/
misoprostol-for-early-abortion-en/, accessed August 30, 2017.
10. Anibal Faundes, "Use of Misoprostol in Obstetrics and Gynaecology,"
*Latin American Federation of Obstetrics and Gynaecology Societies
(FLASOG)* (Santa Cruz, Bolivia: Industrias Gráficas Sirena, April 2005),
www.ibrarian.net/navon/paper/Translated_from_Spanish.pdf.
11. Donna Bowater, "Abortion in Brazil: a Matter of Life and Death," *Guardian*, February 1, 2015, https://www.theguardian.com/world/2015/feb/01
/abortion-in-brazil-a-matter-of-life-and-death, accessed January 23, 2017.
12. See Bela Ganatra et al., "From Concept to Measurement: Operationalizing WHO's Definition of Unsafe Abortion," *Bulletin of the World Health
Organization* 92, no. 155 (2014), doi: http://dx.doi.org/10.2471/BLT.14
.136333 (discussing the definition of "unsafe abortion," in view of factors
ranging from legal context to relative risks depending on access to trained
health care providers and medical abortions).

13. According to the World Health Organization (WHO), Latin America and the Caribbean have the highest regional rate of unsafe abortions per capita in the world (31 per 1,000 women, aged fifteen to forty-four) and see an estimated 4.2 million unsafe abortions every year. See Department of Reproductive Health and Research, World Health Organization, *Unsafe Abortion*.

14. Alejandro Guidos, author interview. For a thorough discussion of these conflicting laws, see Heathe Luz McNaughton et al., "Patient Privacy and Conflicting Legal and Ethical Obligations in El Salvador: Reporting of Unlawful Abortions," *American Journal of Public Health* 96 (2006): 1932.

15. McNaughton et al., "Patient Privacy and Conflicting Legal and Ethical Obligations in El Salvador."

16. For a detailed history of the Hippocratic oath and its ongoing relevance, see Steven H. Miles, *The Hippocratic Oath and the Ethics of Medicine* (Oxford, UK: Oxford University Press, 2004).

17. Raphael Hulkower, "The History of the Hippocratic Oath: Outdated, Inauthentic, and Yet Still Relevant," *Einstein Journal of Biology & Medicine* 25/26 (March 2010): 43, https://www.einstein.yu.edu/uploadedFiles /EJBM/page41_page44.pdf.

18. El Salvador's Health Code 287 states that breaching [patient] confidentiality may result in oral reprimand, written reprimand, a fine, a five-year suspension or the loss of one's medical license. For US law requiring doctors to maintain confidentiality, see Health Insurance Portability and Accountability Act, Pub. L. No. 104–191 (1996), requiring health-care providers and health plans to have policies and procedures concerning use and disclosure of protected health information.

19. Breach of Professional Confidentiality Sect. 187.

20. See Republic of El Salvador, Criminal and Procedural Codes: Prison Law and Its Regulations, Editorial Jurídica Salvadoreña, 2001, Penal Code, Art 312.

21. See Republic of El Salvador, Health Code (with incorporated reforms), Criminal and Procedural Codes: Prison Law and Its Regulations, Editorial Jurídica Salvadoreña, 2001, Penal Code, Art 232. Doctors, pharmacists, nurses, and other health professionals must report unlawful criminal acts that they become aware of in the context of their professional relationship, *unless the information they acquire is protected under the terms of professional secrecy* (translation; italics added).

22. "Miscarriage," *Medline Plus*, reviewed by Cynthia D. White, MD, November 16, 2014, http://www.nlm.nih.gov/medlineplus/ency/article /001488.htm.

23. OBOS Pregnancy & Birth Contributors, "Miscarriage in the First Trimester," *Our Bodies, Our Selves*, April 9, 2014, http://www.ourbodiesourselves.org/health-info/miscarriage-in-the-first-trimester/.

24. As applied in homicide cases, the term *corpus delecti* has at least two component elements: the fact of death, and the criminal act or agency of another person as the cause thereof. "Homicide," *American Jurisprudence*, second ed., section 4.

25. Michelle Oberman, "Cristina's World: Lessons from El Salvador's Ban on Abortion," *Stanford Law and Policy Review* 24 (2013): 271, http://digitalcommons.law.scu.edu/facpubs/794/; Tracy Wilkinson, "El Salvador Jails Women for Miscarriages and Stillbirths," *Los Angeles Times*, April 15, 2015, http://www.latimes.com/world/great-reads/la-fg-c1-el-salvador-women-20150415-story.html.

26. Another study confirmed the disproportionate reporting patterns by doctors treating patients at public hospitals, and suggested three possible explanations. First, public health institutions are more likely to treat indigent women and adolescents who often resort to unsafe, low-cost, and readily detectable abortion methods (e.g., insertion of foreign objects). Second, private-sector providers have an explicit profit motive to protect their individual patients' privacy and avoid legal inconveniences. Finally, because public health-care workers are subject to governmental oversight and are susceptible to shifting ministerial politics, they may be more fearful of reprisal if they do not comply with prevailing governmental ideology or policies. McNaughton et al., "Patient Privacy and Conflicting Legal and Ethical Obligations in El Salvador."

27. Dr. Bernadette Rosario (pseudonym), in discussion with the author, March 2014. Transcription and notes on file with author.

28. Ibid.

29. Samantha Artiga, "Disparities in Health and Health Care: Five Key Questions and Answers," Kaiser Family Foundation, August 12, 2016, http://kff.org/disparities-policy/issue-brief/disparities-in-health-and-health-care-five-key-questions-and-answers/.

30. Details of this case are drawn from the trial transcript, on file with author.

31. Ibid.

32. Dr. Marvin Diaz (pseudonym), in El Salvador, May 23, 2012, in discussion with the author. Transcription and notes on file with the author.

33. Jessica Alpert, "El Salvador Virtual Jewish History Tour," Jewish Virtual Library, http://www.jewishvirtuallibrary.org/el-salvador-virtual-jewish-history-tour#life, accessed May 31, 2017.

34. For a detailed history of Conversos in the Iberian Peninsula, see Norman Roth, *Conversos, Inquisition, and the Expulsion of the Jews from Spain* (Madison: University of Wisconsin Press, 2002); for an analysis of the effect of Conversos on Judaism and Christianity, see also Jose Faur, *In the Shadow of History: Jews and Conversos at the Dawn of Modernity* (Albany: State University of New York Press, 1992).

35. Dr. Marvin Diaz, in discussion with the author. In asserting that the defendant's mother pressed charges against her daughter, Dr. Diaz made the common mistake of confusing civil and criminal charges. Even if her mother had found the baby and called the police, as opposed to simply permitting them to enter and search her apartment, in criminal actions, it is the state that presses criminal charges.

36. Citizen's Coalition for the Decriminalization of Abortion on Grounds of Health, Ethics and Fetal Anomaly, El Salvador, "From Hospital to Jail: The Impact on Women of El Salvador's Total Criminalization of Abortion," *Reproductive Health Matters* 22, no. 44 (2014): 52–60, http://www.rhm-elsevier.com/article/S0968–8080(14)44797–9/fulltext.

37. Ibid. Of women arrested in abortion-related cases, 46.5 percent involved cases of advanced pregnancy and resulted in charges of simple or aggravated homicide.

38. Lauren Bohn, "El Salvador's 'Abortion Lawyer,'" *New York Times*, September 12, 2016, http://kristof.blogs.nytimes.com/2016/09/12/el-salvadors-abortion-lawyer/.

39. See Rebecca G. Stephenson and Linda J. O'Connor, *Obstetric and Gynecologic Care in Physical Therapy*, 2nd ed. (Thorofare, NJ: Slack, 2000).

40. Dr. Anne Drapkin Lyerly, associate professor of social medicine and obstetrics and gynecology, University of North Carolina, in telephone discussion with the author on August 2, 2012.

41. Ibid.

42. To get a sense of the scope of Agrupación Ciudadana activities, see its website, at https://agrupacionCiudadana.org/.

43. Morena Herrera, in discussion with the author, June 2014.

44. Citizens' Coalition for the Decriminalization of Abortion on Grounds of Health, Ethics and Fetal Anomaly, El Salvador, "From Hospital to Jail: The Impact on Women of El Salvador's Total Criminalization of Abortion."

45. The only women excluded were those whose cases were still on appeal, so their sentences were not yet final. Munoz, author interview.

46. Citizen's Coalition for the Decriminalization of Abortion on Grounds of Health, Ethics and Fetal Anomaly, El Salvador, "From Hospital to Jail: The Impact on Women of El Salvador's Total Criminalization of Abortion."

47. Liz Ford, "El Salvador Pardons Woman Jailed After Birth Complications Led to the Death of Child," *Guardian*, January 22, 2015, https://www .theguardian.com/global-development/2015/jan/22/el-salvador-pardons -woman-guadalupe-stillbirth-miscarriage-anti-abortion-laws.

48. Marisela Gloria Moran, "Seis mujeres libres de condenas por aborto," *Contrapunto*, September 20, 2016, http://www.contrapunto.com.sv /sociedad/ddhh/seis-mujeres-libres-de-condenas-por-aborto/1717.

49. "El Salvador: liberan a María Teresa Rivera, condenada a 40 años tras un aborto," *BBC World*, May 21, 2016, http://www.bbc.com/mundo /noticias/2016/05/160520_america_latina_salvador_liberan_maria _teresa_rivera_aborto_dgm.

50. Kathy Bougher, "Salvadoran Council Uses Poverty to Justify Keeping Las 17 in Prison," *Rewire News*, January 7, 2015, https://rewire.news/article /2015/01/07/salvadoran-council-uses-poverty-justify-keeping-las-17-prison/.

51. As translated in *The Portable Nietzsche*, ed. Walter Kaufmann (New York: Viking, 1954), 458.

52. Nina Strochlic, "On the Front Lines of El Salvador's Underground Abortion Economy," *Foreign Policy*, January 3, 2017, http://foreignpolicy.com /2017/01/03/on-the-front-lines-of-el-salvadors-underground-abortion -economy/.

53. Twenty-four percent of pregnancies occurred in women from fifteen to nineteen years old. The specific fertility rate of women from fifteen to nineteen years old was eighty-nine per one thousand. Seven of ten adolescents with sexual experience had a pregnancy, and 8.9 percent of this group had had a previous pregnancy. See Pan American Health Organization, "Health in the Americas: El Salvador," 2012, http://www.paho.org /salud-en-las-americas-2012/index.php?option=com_content&view =article&id=36%3Ael-salvador&catid=21%3Acountry-chapters&Itemid =145&lang=en.

54. Anastasia Moloney, "Rape, Abortion Ban Drives Pregnant Teens to Suicide in El Salvador," Reuters Health News, November 12, 2014, http:// www.reuters.com/article/us-el-salvador-suicide-teens-idUSKCN0IW1Y I20141112.

55. Carlos Mayora, in discussion with the author, June 5, 2014.

56. This description is taken from the facts of "Manuela's case," which resulted in an appeal to the InterAmerican Court of Human Rights in Peru. She died in prison of cancer, which the prison doctors misdiagnosed and failed to treat. Charlotte Krol, "Are El Salvador's Extreme Anti-Abortion Laws Justified?," *Telegraph*, February 14, 2015, http://www.telegraph.co.uk/news/worldnews/centralamericaandthecaribbean/elsalvador/11412550/Are-El-Salvadors-extreme-anti-abortion-laws-justified.html.
57. See Ferguson v. City of Charleston, 532 U.S. 67 (2001) (holding that a urine test conducted by the hospital in conjunction with law enforcement absent the patient's consent was a violation of the Fourth Amendment right to be free from unreasonable searches). The use of criminal sanctions in the public hospital setting disproportionately affects poor, minority women. See, generally, Dorothy E. Roberts, "Punishing Drug Addicts Who Have Babies: Women of Color, Equality, and the Right of Privacy," *Harvard Law Review* 104 (1991): 1419 (arguing that given the historical context of devaluing black mothers, prosecuting these women violates their equal protection and privacy rights regarding reproductive choices); Michele Goodwin, "Prosecuting the Womb," *George Washington Law Review* 76 (2008): 1657, 1661 (describing how fetal drug laws are inconsistent, ineffective, and exempt reproductive practices by affluent groups that are equally risky to the unborn fetus).

Chapter 3: The Reddest State

1. See CNN Election Center 2008, http://www.cnn.com/ELECTION/2008/results/individual/#mapPOK and Politico's 2012; Oklahoma Presidential Results, http://www.politico.com/2012-election/results/president/oklahoma/, last updated 11/19/12.
2. The AUL's Life List report card is compiled by looking at abortion-related measures by state. Four states earned AUL's 2017 All-Star Status for their implementation of legislation written by AUL. See AUL's 2017 Life List, http://www.aul.org/2017-life-list/.
3. Joshua Holland, "When Southern Baptists Were Pro-Choice," *Moyers & Co.*, July 2014, http://billmoyers.com/2014/07/17/when-southern-baptists-were-pro-choice/.
4. Edward Lee Pitts, "Successful State Strategies Saving Babies," *The World*, January 22, 2014, https://world.wng.org/2014/01/successful_state_strategies_saving_babies.
5. In 1910, Tony Lauinger's ancestor founded PennWell Corporation, a privately held company in the fifth generation of continuous family

ownership. The company today has over 600 employees across offices worldwide, with 343 at its headquarters in Tulsa. His family has endowed Georgetown University with a Library Fund to foster Catholic values through the acquisition of current and retrospective books, journals, periodicals, audio-visuals, computer archives, and other library materials supportive of the teachings of Magisterium on the issues of abortion, contraception, infanticide, homosexuality, assisted suicide, euthanasia, reproductive technologies, and other similar issues related to marriage, family, human sexuality, human life, and bioethics.

6. Kristen Luker, *Abortion and the Politics of Motherhood* (Berkeley: University of California Press, 1984).
7. Ibid., 128.
8. For details about the paper and its circulation, see http://www.baptist messenger.com.
9. Chris Doyle, "Rose Day at 25," *Baptist Messenger*, February 3, 2016, https://www.baptistmessenger.com/rose-day-at-25/.
10. Bernest Cain, in discussion with the author, July 2013.
11. Andrew Spiropoulus, in discussion with the author, June 2013.
12. See "Timeline: Oklahoma Abortion Legislation at a Glance," *Oklahoman*, November 4, 2013, http://newsok.com/article/3901078.
13. For a detailed overview of Trisomy 18, see http://www.trisomy18.org /what-is-trisomy-18/.
14. Mike Reynolds, in discussion with the author, June 2013.
15. Ryan Kiesel, in discussion with the author, June 2013.
16. "Tom Smith," in discussion with the author, June 2013.
17. Kiesel, author interview.
18. Kris Steele, in discussion with the author, June 2013.

Chapter 4: The Abortion-Minded Woman and the Law

1. Lawrence Finer, Lori Frohwirth, Lindsay Dauphinee, Susheela Singh, and Ann Moore, "Reasons US Women Have Abortions: Quantitative and Qualitative Perspectives," *Perspectives on Sexual and Reproductive Health* 37 no. 3 (2005): 110–18, http://www.guttmacher.org/pubs/psrh /full/3711005.pdf.
2. Adoption lurks in the corners of any serious conversation about abortion, and I recognized Chisko's tacit reference to it here. I don't discuss adoption in this book. In a world where abortion is legal, issues surrounding adoption—its regulation, its impact on all those involved—are only tangentially relevant. Were abortion to become illegal, relinquishing a

child for adoption would be the only legal way to avoid motherhood. In that world, adoption and its consequences would be at the heart of the conversation.

3. CBS/AP, "California to End Contentious 'Maximum Family Grant' Welfare Policy," *CBS SF Bay Area*, June 14, 2016, http://sanfrancisco .cbslocal.com/2016/06/14/california-end-contentious-maximum-family -grant-welfare/.

4. Jamelle Bouie, "The Most Discriminatory Law in the Land," *Slate*, June 17, 2014, http://www.slate.com/articles/news_and_politics/politics/2014 /06/the_maximum_family_grant_and_family_caps_a_racist_law_that _punishes_the.html.

5. Christine Jolls, Cass Sunstein, and Richard Thaler, "A Behavioral Approach to Law and Economics," *Stanford Law Review* 50 (1998): 471.

6. Dan Kahan, "Gentle Nudges v. Hard Shoves: Solving the Sticky Norms Problem," *University of Chicago Law Review* 67 (2000): 607.

7. Ibid., 626.

8. "Since the Hyde Amendment passed, only four states have voluntarily decided to use their funds to cover abortion. Another thirteen states are required to do so by court order, just as they would other forms of health care. Thirty-two states and the District of Columbia basically follow the Hyde Amendment as the congressman intended, with some small variations. One state, South Dakota, only pays for abortion when a woman's life is in danger, but not in cases of rape and incest—an apparent violation of federal law." See John Light, "Five Facts You Should Know About the Hyde Amendment," *Moyers & Company*, January 25, 2013, http:// billmoyers.com/content/five-facts-you-should-know-about-the-hyde -amendment/.

9. Tribune News Service, "Democrats Seek Repeal of Ban on Federal Funding of Abortion," *Chicago Tribune*, August 16, 2016, http://www .chicagotribune.com/news/nationworld/ct-abortion-federal-funding-ban -20160816-story.html.

10. Rebecca Blank, Christine George, and Rebecca London, "State Abortion Rates: The Impact of Policies, Providers, Politics, Demographics, and Economic Environment," NBER Working Paper No. 4853 (September 1994), http://www.nber.org/papers/w4853.

11. Post-*Roe* laws from "Timeline of Abortion Laws and Events," *Chicago Tribune*, http://www.chicagotribune.com/sns-abortion-timeline-story. html: "1976—Congress passes the Hyde Amendment, banning the use of Medicaid and other federal funds for abortions. The legislation is

upheld by the Supreme Court in 1980. 1979—A Missouri requirement
that abortions after the first trimester be performed in hospitals is found
unconstitutional. Another law mandating parental consent is upheld.
1981—In *Bellotti v. Baird*, Supreme Court rules that pregnant minors
can petition court for permission to have an abortion without parental
notification. 1983—The court strikes down an Akron ordinance that requires doctors to give abortion patients antiabortion literature, imposes
a 24-hour waiting period, requires abortions after the first trimester to
be performed in a hospital, requires parental consent and requires the
aborted fetus to be disposed of in a human manner. 1989—In *Webster
v. Reproductive Health Services*, a law in Washington State declaring
that 'life begins at conception' and barring the use of public facilities for
abortions is found unconstitutional. It marks the first time the Supreme
Court does not explicitly reaffirm *Roe v. Wade*. 1992—In *Planned Parenthood v. Casey*, the court reaffirms *Roe*'s core holding that states may
not ban abortions or interfere with a woman's decision to have an abortion. The court does uphold mandatory 24-hour waiting periods and
parental-consent laws."

12. *Planned Parenthood of Southeastern Pennsylvania v. Casey*, 505 U.S. 833
(1992).

13. Ibid., 878.

14. Niraj Chokshi, "Abortion Doctors Would Lose Medical Licenses Under
New Oklahoma Bill," *Washington Post*, April 23, 2016, https://www
.washingtonpost.com/news/morning-mix/wp/2016/04/23/this-is-our-proper
-function-oklahoma-advances-measure-to-revoke-licenses-of-doctors-that
-perform-abortions/?utm_term=.40a7b2951ca9.

15. The Data Team, "The Abortion Rate in America Falls to Its Lowest Level
since Roe v. Wade," *Economist*, January 18, 2017, http://www.economist
.com/blogs/graphicdetail/2017/01/daily-chart-16.

16. See debates between Michael New, Marshall Medoff, and Christopher
Dennis; Michael New, "Analyzing the Effect of Anti-Abortion U.S. State
Legislation in the Post Casey Era," *State Politics and Policy Quarterly*
11 (2011): 28–47; Marshall Medoff and Christopher Dennis, "Another
Critical Review of New's Reanalysis of the Impact of Antiabortion Legislation," *State Politics & Policy Quarterly* 14, no. 3 (2014): 207–27;
Marshall Medoff, "Biased Abortion Counseling Laws and Abortion Demand," *Social Science Journal* 46 (2009): 632–43, https://www.infona
.pl/resource/bwmeta1.element.elsevier-141efa1a-29c3–3dfa-83f9–73903
a82b670/tab/summary.

17. Sarah Roberts, David Turok, Elise Belusa, Sarah Combellick, and Ushma Upadhyay, "Utah's 72-Hour Waiting Period for Abortion: Experiences Among a Clinic-Based Sample of Women," *Perspectives on Sexual and Reproductive Health* 48 no. 4 (2016): 179–87, doi: 10.1363/48e8216.

18. Erica Hellerstein and Tara Culp-Ressler, "Pricing American Women out of Abortion, One Restriction at a Time," *ThinkProgress*, February 25, 2015, https://thinkprogress.org/pricing-american-women-out-of-abortion-one -restriction-at-a-time-c545c54f641f#.jzr6c8z64.

Chapter 5: America After *Roe*

1. Jeffrey Antevil, "Supreme Court Rules on Roe vs. Wade in 1973," *New York Daily News*, January 21, 2015, http://www.nydailynews.com/news /national/supreme-court-rules-roe-v-wade-1973-article-1.2068726.

2. Constitutional Amendment Process, National Archives, August 15, 2016, https://www.archives.gov/federal-register/constitution. For a time, the pro-life movement threw its support into campaigning for such a change in the form of the "Human Life Amendment." Although the Republican Party's platform continues to support the Human Life Amendment, the movement has had little traction in Congress. It has been decades since Congress even considered the issue. See the Human Life Action website for an account of activity on the Human Life Amendment, https://www .humanlifeaction.org/sites/default/files/HLAhghlts.pdf.

3. Pete Williams, "Abortion Could Be Outlawed in 33 States if *Roe v. Wade* Overturned: Report," *NBC News*, January 23, 2017, http://www.nbc news.com/news/us-news/report-abortion-could-be-outlawed-33-states-if -roe-v-n710816.

4. "Marina," in discussion with the author, 2009.

5. Seth F. Kreimer, *The Law of Choice and Choice of Law: Abortion, the Right to Travel, and Extraterritorial Regulation in American Federalism* (1992), Faculty Scholarship Paper, 1336fn9, http://scholarship.law.upenn .edu/faculty_scholarship/1336.

6. See Colleen Heild, "New Mexico Becomes Abortion Magnet," *Albuquerque Journal*, March 20, 2016, https://www.abqjournal.com/743253/more -women-coming-to-nm-for-abortions.html.

7. See Kate Sheppard, "Why This Woman Chose Abortion—at 29 Weeks," *Mother Jones*, July 25, 2011, http://www.motherjones.com/politics/2011 /07/late-term-abortion-29-weeks-dana-weinstein; also see Molly Hennessy-Fiske, "Crossing the 'Abortion Desert': Women Increasingly Travel out of Their States for the Procedure," *Los Angeles Times*, June 2, 2016, http://

www.latimes.com/nation/la-na-adv-abortion-traveler-20160530-snap
-story.html.

8. Compare with Mark D. Rosen, "Extraterritoriality and Political Hetero-
geneity in American Federalism," *University of Pennsylvania Law Review*
150 (2002): 855, http://scholarship.law.upenn.edu/penn_law_review
/vol150/iss3/2. Rosen argues that the law actually permits states to regulate their citizens' out-of-state activities for the purpose of ensuring the
efficacy of constitutional state policies, and that state's determinations
to regulate citizens' extraterritorial conduct is actually only a policy
decision.

9. Alan Guttmacher Institute, "Abortion in Africa: Incidence and Trends,"
May 2016, https://www.guttmacher.org/fact-sheet/facts-abortion-africa.

10. Andrew Downie, "Abortions in Brazil, Though Illegal, Are Common," *Time*,
June 2, 2010, http://content.time.com/time/world/article/0,8599,1993205,00
.html.

11. Texas Policy Evaluation Project, "Texas Women's Experiences Attempting
Self-Induced Abortion in the Face of Dwindling Options," November 17,
2015, https://liberalarts.utexas.edu/txpep/_files/pdf/TxPEP-Research-Brief
-WomensExperiences.pdf.

12. See Tess Barker, "The New Reality: Women Charged for Murder After
Self-Inducing Abortions," *Broadly*, January 24, 2016, https://broadly.vice
.com/en_us/article/the-new-reality-women-charged-for-murder-after-self
-inducing-abortions. Also see Teresa A. Saultes, Diane Devita, and
Jason D. Heiner, "The Back Alley Revisited: Sepsis after Attempted
Self-Induced Abortion," *Western Journal of Emergency Medicine* 10,
no. 4 (2009): 278–80.

13. Paltrow, "*Roe v. Wade* and the New Jane Crow," 17–21. A 2010 case from
Utah involved a woman charged with illegal abortion after hiring a man to
beat her up in order to bring on a miscarriage.

14. Matt Flegenheimer and Maggie Haberman, "Donald Trump, Abortion
Foe, Eyes 'Punishment' for Women, Then Recants," *New York Times*,
March 30, 2016, https://www.nytimes.com/2016/03/31/us/politics
/donald-trump-abortion.html; Tara Culp-Ressler, "Abortion Bans Are
Putting Women Behind Bars," *ThinkProgress*, March 9, 2015, https://
thinkprogress.org/abortion-bans-are-putting-women-behind-bars
-119b8fba1c70.

15. Rachel Lu, "Why Pro-Lifers Don't Support Punishing Women for Abortion," *Federalist*, April 5, 2016, http://thefederalist.com/2016/04/05/why
-pro-lifers-dont-support-punishing-women-for-abortion/.

16. Flegenheimer and Haberman, "Donald Trump, Abortion Foe." The day after Donald Trump's remarks, the *New York Times* reported on the outpouring of condemnation by pro-life advocates throughout the country. The article quoted Jeanne Mancini, the president of the March for Life Education Fund, as saying that efforts to punish individual women would be "completely out of touch with the pro-life movement" and "no pro-lifer would ever want to punish a woman who has chosen abortion"; Bruce Haynes, a Republican strategist, as stating he could not recall "'any credible corner of the movement' calling for criminal sanctions against women who sought abortions"; Governor John Kasich as declaring, "Of course women shouldn't be punished"; and Senator Ted Cruz as stating, with reference to a woman who has an abortion, "Of course we shouldn't be talking about punishment."
17. Clarke Forsythe, "Why the States Did Not Prosecute Women for Abortion Before *Roe v. Wade*," Americans United for Life, April 23, 2010, http://www.aul.org/2010/04/why-the-states-did-not-prosecute-women -for-abortion-before-roe-v-wade/.
18. Reagan, *When Abortion Was a Crime*.
19. Ibid., 114, 164.
20. Leslie Reagan, "Victim or Accomplice? Crime, Medical Malpractice, and the Construction of the Aborting Women in American Case Law, 1860s–1970," *Columbia Journal of Gender and Law* 10 (2001): 311, 332. "Although state laws provided for the prosecution of women who had abortions, late-nineteenth-century state prosecutors went after the abortionists. Juries were reluctant, however, to convict people accused of performing abortions. As a result, prosecutors increasingly focused on prosecuting abortionists whose practice had resulted in the death or severe injury of a woman patient. This emphasis did not change until around 1940 (332).
21. Samuel W. Buell, "Criminal Abortion Revisited," *New York University Law Review* 66 (1991): 1774, 1785.
22. Suzanne M. Alford, "Is Self-Abortion a Fundamental Right?," *Duke Law Journal* 52 (2003): 1011, 1022. New York, Laws of 1869, Chap. 631, entitled "An act relating to the procurement of abortions, and other like offences": Every woman who shall solicit of any person any medicine, drug, or substance or thing whatever, and shall take the same, or shall submit to any operation, or other means whatever, with intent thereby to procure a miscarriage, shall be deemed guilty of a misdemeanor, and shall, upon conviction, be punished by imprisonment in the county jail, not less than

three months nor more than one year, or by a fine not exceeding one thousand dollars, or by both such fine and imprisonment.

23. Louisiana, Mississippi, and North and South Dakota have laws in place that would automatically make abortion illegal if *Roe v. Wade* were to be overturned. Pete Williams, "Abortion Could Be Outlawed in 33 States if *Roe v. Wade* Overturned: Report," *NBC News*, January 23, 2017, http://www.nbcnews.com/news/us-news/report-abortion-could-be-outlawed-33 -states-if-roe-v-n710816.

24. See *Commonwealth v. Weible*, 45 Pa. Super. 207 (1911). Also see Crissman v. State, 93 Tex. Crim. 15, 245 S.W. 438 (Tex. Crim. App. 1922).

25. Carmen Hein de Campos, "Mass Prosecution for Abortion: Violation of the Reproductive Rights of Women in Mato Grosso do Sul, Brazil," AWID Women's Rights, 2016, https://www.oursplatform.org/resource /mass-prosecution-abortion-violation-reproductive-rights-women-mato -grosso-sul-brazil/.

26. "Abortion Prosecutions on the Rise in Many Mexican States," *Mexico Gulf Reporter*, August 6, 2012, http://mexicogulfreporter.blogspot.com /2012/08/abortion-prosecutions-on-rise-in-many.html.

27. Center for Reproductive Rights and the Agrupación Ciudadana, *Marginalized, Persecuted, and Imprisoned: The Effects of El Salvador's Total Criminalization of Abortion* (New York: 2014, https://www.reproductive rights.org/sites/crr.civicactions.net/files/documents/El-Salvador -CriminalizationOfAbortion-Report.pdf.

28. Hadley Arkes, "One Untrue Thing: Life after Roe," National Review Symposium, August 1, 2007, http://www.nationalreview.com/article /221742/one-untrue-thing-nro-symposium.

29. Lynn Paltrow and Jeanne Flavin, "Arrests of and Forced Interventions on Pregnant Women in the United States, 1973–2005: Implications for Women's Legal Status and Public Health," *Journal of Health Politics, Policy and Law* 38, no. 2 (2013): 299–343, http://jhppl.dukejournals.org /content/38/2/299.refs.

30. L. M. Paltrow, "*Roe v. Wade* and the New Jane Crow: Reproductive Rights in the Age of Mass Incarceration," *American Journal of Public Health* 103, no. 1 (2013): 17–21, doi:10.2105/AJPH.2012.301104.

31. Ibid.

32. Five states have laws explicitly criminalizing self-abortion. The other states use alternative theories to bring charges against women. For example, thirty-nine states make it illegal for anyone other than a medical provider to perform the procedure. Although some states explicitly exempt

women from prosecution under state abortion laws, others are silent. As such, whether under self-abortion statutes or under laws restricting abortion to medical providers, women can be and have been charged with illegal abortion.

33. Sally Koh, "Indiana's Other Outrageous Law," CNN, March 31, 2015, http://www.cnn.com/2015/03/31/opinions/kohn-indiana-anti-abortion -law/. Prosecutors claimed that Patel ordered abortion-inducing drugs online and tried to terminate her pregnancy, but a toxicology report failed to find evidence of any drugs in her system. She received a thirty-year-sentence on the felony neglect charge, ten of which were suspended. A six-year sentence for feticide was to be served concurrently. Emily Bazelon, "Purvi Patel Could Be Just the Beginning," *New York Times*, April 1, 2015, https://www.nytimes.com/2015/04/01/magazine/purvi-patel-could-be -just-the-beginning.html.

34. Calvin Freiburger, "Death, Lies, And Relativism in the Purvi Patel Feticide Conviction," *Live Action News*, April 3, 2015, http://liveactionnews.org /death-lies-relativism-purvi-patel-feticide-conviction/.

35. Ibid.

36. Ibid. "The 33-year-old Patel is 'an educated woman of considerable means,' and 'if [she] wished to terminate [her] pregnancy safely and legally, [she] could have done so.' Instead, she repeatedly rejected a friend's insistence that she see a doctor, simply because she didn't want her traditional Hindu parents to know she'd had sex with a married co-worker. She didn't get a doctor to do it, but killed her son herself. Her son who was viable." See also, Texas Right to Life staff, "What Really Happened to Purvi Patel's Baby Boy?," *Texas Right to Life News*, April 9, 2015, https://www.texasrighttolife.com/what-really-happened-to-purvi-patel-s -baby-boy/. "Now, the liberal media's spin on the story goes something like this: Purvi Patel suffered a miscarriage and was thrown in jail for something completely out of her control because Pro-Life feticide laws are *that* outrageous. Cue the evidence-spinning and abortion lobby pandemonium."

37. Associated Press, "Indiana Court Tosses Purvi Patel's 2015 Feticide Conviction," *NBC News*, July 22, 2016, http://www.nbcnews.com/news /asian-america/indiana-court-tosses-purvi-patel-s-2015-feticide-conviction -n615026.

38. Paltrow and Flavin, "Arrests of and Forced Interventions on Pregnant Women," 309.

39. Ibid., 309–10.

40. Ibid., 311.
41. Ibid., 311.
42. Tara Culp-Ressler, "This Woman Says She Had a Miscarriage. Now She Could Face 70 Years in Prison," *ThinkProgress*, March 30, 2015, https://thinkprogress.org/this-woman-says-she-had-a-miscarriage-now-she-could-face-70-years-in-prison-c62d73ba32e1. "According to a study conducted by NAPW reviewing the prosecutions of women in relation to their pregnancies between 1973 and 2005, low-income women and women of color are disproportionately arrested under feticide laws. Black women are significantly more likely to be reported to authorities by hospital staff under suspicion that they harmed their unborn children."
43. "Twelve Facts About the Abortion Ban in El Salvador," *Amnesty International Report*, September 25, 2014, https://www.amnesty.org/en/latest/news/2014/09/twelve-facts-about-abortion-ban-el-salvador/. El Salvador has the highest rate of teenage pregnancy in Latin America. According to the National Family Health Survey, more than one-fifth (23 percent) of all teenagers aged between fifteen and nineteen in El Salvador have been pregnant at least once. Nearly half of them were under eighteen and didn't intend to get pregnant.
44. Ibid. Suicide accounts for 57 percent of the deaths of pregnant females aged ten to nineteen in El Salvador, though it is likely many more cases have gone unreported.
45. Moloney, "Rape, Abortion Ban Drives Pregnant Teens to Suicide."
46. Sunstein, "On the Expressive Function of Law," 2021, 2031.

Conclusion: Parting Thoughts on Leaving Behind the Abortion War

1. George Orwell. "Looking Back on the Spanish War" (1943), reprinted in *A Collection of Essays* (New York: Harcourt, 1946), 193–94.

INDEX

abortion: ban on, in Chile (*see* Chile); ban on, in El Salvador (*see* El Salvador); debate on (*see* abortion debate); doctrine of double-effect and, 32, 149*n*29; fetal status as a separate human being and, 31; impact of bans on the abortion rate, 44, 63; impact of bans on the birth rate, 63–64; laws against (*see* abortion laws); legal battles in the 1990s, 4; misinformation about oral contraceptives, 83–84; moral boundaries expressed in abortion bans, 41; potential medical consequences of a surgical abortion, 44–45; public choice theory and opposition to, 92–93; rates of maternal mortality from, 8, 124, 146n8; reasons women choose, 1–2; relevance of abortion's legal status for vulnerable women, 4–5, 6–7, 11; state-mandated misinformation about, 145–46n5; symbolic laws and, 41–42, 141–42; in the US (*see* United States); women's consideration of the laws concerning (*see* abortion-minded women)
Abortion and the Politics of Motherhood (Luker), 71
abortion debate: common ground in, 141–42; emotions embedded on both sides of, 139–40; fetal status as a separate human being and, 31; fundamental rights for women and, 36; moral boundaries expressed in

abortion bans, 3, 41, 81, 83–84, 85; pro-life versus antiabortion, 103; symbolic importance of abortion laws, 41–42, 141
abortion drugs, 8, 45–46, 124, 125, 151n8
abortion laws: anti-abortion activists' vision for, 79; in Chile (*see* Chile); constitutionality of states' anti-abortion laws, 114, 120, 122, 158–59*n*11; correlation between abortion rates and, 44, 114–15; doctors' compliance with (*see* doctors and abortion detection); in El Salvador (*see* El Salvador); impact on poor women, 66, 75, 78–79, 113, 115–16, 117, 123, 156*n*57; intent of, 113, 116–17; moral justification derived from, 137; questioning if the laws matter, 12; against self-abortion, 128, 131, 162–63*nn*22–23, 163*n*32; symbolic importance of, 41–42, 141; in the US (*see* United States)
abortion-minded women: constitutionality of states' anti-abortion laws, 114, 120, 122, 158–59*n*11; cost factor of motherhood, 97–98, 106, 107, 109–11; crisis pregnancy centers and, 99 (*see also* Birth Choice); de facto fertility policy in the US, 109–11; family caps on welfare recipients, 110–11; impact of abortion laws on poor women, 66, 75, 78–79, 113, 115–16, 117, 123, 156*n*57; impact of public policy

choices on, 111; impact of restrictive laws on abortion rates, 114–15; impact of *Roe* on choices made, 112; intent of anti-abortion laws, 113, 116–17; lawmakers' capacity to shape human behavior, 112; lawmakers' testing of their power to regulate abortion, 113; monetary impact of abortion restrictions, 115–16; pregnancy's impact on existing vulnerabilities for poor women, 1–2, 3–4, 108–9; pro-life states' responses to "undue burden test," 114; pro-motherhood intent of abortion laws, 113; relevancy of abortion's legal status for vulnerable women, 4–5, 6–7, 11; Western European policies that encourage childbearing, 109

abortion tourism, 123
Access Women's Health Justice (AWHJ), 107–8, 110, 141
adoption, 157–58n2
Africa, 124
Agrupación Ciudadana, 61
Americans United for Life (AUL), 70, 78, 114, 127, 156n2
Amnesty International, 26
anencephaly, 17
Aquinas, Thomas, 149n29
ARENA, 22
Arizona, 145–46n5
Arkes, Hadley, 129
Azam-Yu, Samara, 107–9, 110, 111

Baptist Children's Home, 72
Baptist Messenger, 72
Beatriz's story. *See* petition for an abortion in El Salvador
Bellotti v. Baird, 159n11
Big Sort, The (Bishop), 90
Birth Choice, 141; background and founders, 99–102; choice of residents for their safe house, 105; counselors' sentiments about why a woman would hurt her child, 101; founding story, 102–3; mission, 103, 106;

position on a complete ban on abortion, 106; supportive services, 101, 103–5, 106
Bishop, Bill, 90
black market abortions, 123–26
Blakely, Ruth, 102. *See also* Birth Choice
Brazil, 45, 124, 128

Cain, Bernest, 70–71, 75–76, 78
California, 107, 110
Cardenal, Julia Regina de, 26–27
Casas, Lidia, 7–9
Catholic Church, 23, 32, 71, 73, 74, 91, 149n29
Chile: cost of an abortion, 9; enacting of the abortion ban, 7–8; number of drug-induced abortions per year, 8, 146n7; prosecutions for abortions, 8–9, 127; rates of maternal mortality from abortions, 8, 146n8; results of convictions for obtaining an abortion, 9–10; use of abortion drugs in, 8
Chisko, Barbara, 100. *See also* Birth Choice
Christina's story: delivery of her baby, 57; police response to a doctor's report, 58; probability that she experienced a medical emergency, 58, 59; prosecutor's argument at the preliminary hearing, 58; release due to a judicial error, 60; reopening of her case with new charges, 59
coat hangers and abortion, 45, 64, 119, 123, 126
contraception, 1, 3, 44, 83–84, 136, 139
corpus delicti, 49, 153n23
crisis pregnancy centers, 99. *See also* Birth Choice
Cruz, Ted, 162n16
Cytotec, 125

Death Peddlers, The (Marx), 106
District of Colombia, 158n8
doctors and abortion detection: case of feticide and child neglect charge, 132–33, 164n33, 164n36; diagnostic

challenge of distinguishing abortion from miscarriage, 48–49, 52; doctors' compliance with reporting suspected abortions, 49–50, 51, 153n26; a doctor's support of the abortion law, 53–54; government's enlistment of doctors, 46; legal process for pressing charges, 53, 154n35; legal standard for proving a crime, 49, 153n23; patient confidentiality imperative and, 46–48, 50, 51, 53, 54, 152n17, 152n20; percentage of Salvadorans who go to private doctors, 50–51; poor women's options for medical care, 51; portrayal of medical confidentiality as a commodity, 50, 53; reporting by private versus public hospitals, 50, 153n26; sources of reports triggering prosecutions, 49–50, 52
doctrine of double-effect, 23, 32, 149n29
drug addiction. See pregnant addicts

ectopic pregnancies, 18–19
Education and Employment Ministry, The (TEEM), 89
El Salvador: abortion drugs availability and efficacy, 45; abortion law's effect on wealthy women, 65; addressing of wrongful convictions, 60–62; anti-abortionists' focus on the fetus, 65; arrests made after hospital admission, 10; availability of documentation of abortion prosecutions, 52; basis for overturned convictions, 62; case of an abortion petition (see petition for an abortion in El Salvador); constitution's position on when life begins, 30–31; correlation between abortion rates and abortion laws, 44; doctors' role in reporting abortions (see doctors and abortion detection); dominant religious affiliations of citizens, 23; focus on arresting women, 128–29; goal of abortion-rights activists, 61; impact of abortion ban on the birth rate, 63–64; influence of

a women's socioeconomic status on accusations, 65–66, 156n56; investigation of women for abortion-related offenses, 55; legal distinction between abortion and homicide, 56, 154n37; legal standard for proving a crime, 49, 153n23; legislative assembly's rejection of pardons, 63; moral boundaries expressed in the abortion ban, 41; number of illegal abortions every year, 44; passing of the law banning abortion, 43; patient confidentiality laws, 47, 152n17, 152n20; petitions filed to overturn abortion-related homicide, 61; potential medical consequences of a surgical abortion, 44–45; pregnant-teen suicide rate, 136–37, 165n44; pressing of charges in a criminal case, 53, 154n35; rates of unsafe abortions, 45–46, 152n12; restrictions on treating ectopic pregnancies, 18–19; scope of its abortion ban, 17; socioeconomic status' role in the risks of illegal abortion, 64, 125; suicides among pregnant teens, 64; targeting of the poor in public hospitals, 66, 156n57; teen pregnancies and, 64, 136, 165nn43–44; unwed teen birth rate, 64, 155n53; wrongful convictions of women, 52–53, 55, 57–60

Farabundo Martí National Liberation Front (FMLN), 22
Faundes, Anibal, 27
Ferguson v. City of Charleston, 156n57
feticide. See women who killed their children
Fiscalia de la Republica, 17
Flavin, Jeanne, 130, 135
Florida, 134
Forsythe, Clarke, 127
Fortin Magana, Jose Miguel, 21–26
Funes, Mauricio, 26

Garcia, Sara, 36–38
gay rights, 75

Gordy, Katie, 100. *See also* Birth Choice
Grossman, Dan, 125
Guidos, Alejandro, 46, 148*n*16

H&H Shooting Sports, 82
Handbook on Abortion (Wilke), 106
Haynes, Bruce, 162*n*16
Hellman, Lawrence, 70
Herrera, Morena, 61
Hippocratic oath, 47, 52
Homage to Catalonia (Orwell), 140
Hope Pregnancy Center, 74
Human Life Amendment, 160*n*11
Human Life International, 26
Hyde Amendment, 113, 158*n*11, 158*n*13

infanticide. *See* women who killed their
    children
Instituto de Medicina Legal (IML):
    criteria for permitting an abortion,
    21; examination of Beatriz, 25–26;
    experts assembled by, 22–24; status
    and staffing, 21–22
InterAmerican Court of Human Rights,
    156*n*56

Johnson, Constance, 89
Jordan, Anthony, 72–73, 79, 89

Kahan, Dan, 112
Karina's story, 52–53, 55
Kasich, John, 162*n*16
Kern, Sally, 84
Kiesel, Ryan, 85, 88–89

La Maternidad, 16
Latin America, 45–46, 124, 151*n*8. *See
    also* Chile; El Salvador
Lauinger, Tony: contribution to pro-life
    education, 156–57*n*5; influence over
    the legislature, 80–81, 82, 84, 85,
    89; power over the political process,
    70; pro-life activism beginnings, 71,
    156–57*n*5; refusal to meet with a
    pro-choice person, 79–81, 140
law of self-defense, 34–35

LeFrancois, Arthur, 70
Louisiana, 163*n*23
Luker, Kristen, 71
lupus, 16
Lyerly, Anne Drapkin, 58, 59

Malta, 10
Mancini, Jeanne, 162*n*16
Marx, Paul, 106
maternal health exception, 17, 86–87
maternal mortality rates, 8, 124, 146*n*8
Mayora, Carlos, 29, 31, 32–34, 65
Merchant, Rae, 100. *See also* Birth Choice
Mexico, 128
Mifeprex, 45
mifepristone, 45
miscarriage: distinguishing abortion from,
    46, 48–49, 52, 65; drug induced, 8;
    percent of pregnancies ending in, 125;
    self-induced, 44; wrongful convictions
    and, 56, 58, 61, 62, 131, 133
misoprostol: efficacy of, 45; popularity
    in Latin America, 151*n*8; use of in
    Chile, 8
Mississippi, 163*n*23
Missouri, 134
Molina, Ramiro, 8
Munoz, Dennis, 49, 56, 60, 61

National Right to Life Committee
    (NRLC), 71
Nicaragua, 10
North Dakota, 163*n*23

Oklahoma: abortion's unifying ef-
    fect on the Republican Party, 77;
    anti-abortion activists' vision for
    the new laws, 79; anti-abortionists'
    activities, 82; AUL rating for the
    legislature, 70; Cain's career, 75–76,
    78; centrality of organized religion in
    public life, 72; consideration of the
    impact of abortion laws on women,
    93–94; cost factor in abortion, 79, 87;
    counseling by faith-based organiza-
    tions, 74; "culture of abortion" and,

82–84; evidence of increased homogeneity of American communities, 90;
history of supporting legalized abortion, 70–71; Lauinger's influence over
the legislature, 70, 80–81, 82, 84, 85,
89; Lauinger's pro-life activism, 71,
156–57n5; Lauinger's refusal to meet
with a pro-choice person, 79–81, 140;
lawmakers' view of the purpose of
abortion laws, 85–86, 87, 94; level of
consideration of the likely impact of a
ban, 86, 87, 93; misinformation about
oral contraceptives, 83–84; moral
basis for opposition to abortion, 81,
83–84, 85; new term limits law's
effect on the legislative agenda, 77;
opposition to the "maternal health exception," 86–87; Personhood Act, 84,
85, 92; political leanings in elections,
69; political power of constituent
groups, 75; positions on exemptions
for rape, 87; power of single-issue advocacy, 92–93; power of the pro-life
movement to influence people, 87;
predictions of the political impact of
a reversal of Roe, 88–89, 93; pro-life
activists' alliance with faith-based
communities, 72; restrictive abortion
laws' impact on poor women, 75,
78–79; Reynolds' motivation for
his political service, 81–84; SBC's
involvement in abortion politics,
72–74; Steele's legislative record, 91;
volume of anti-abortion laws passed
after 2006, 77–78; work of a crisis
pregnancy center (see Birth Choice)
Oklahomans for Life, 71
Oklahoma Right to Life, 72
oral contraceptives. See contraception
Organization for the Family, 20
Ortiz, Guillermo, 16, 17–18
Ortiz, Melissa, 110
Orwell, George, 140

Paltrow, Lynn, 130, 135
Pan American Health Organization, 64

Patel, Nareshkumar, 82
Patel, Purvi, 132–33, 164n33, 164n36
patient confidentiality: adherence to by
private practices, 50, 51, 53; imperative of for doctors, 46–48, 53, 54,
152n17, 152n20; portrayal of medical
confidentiality as a commodity, 50, 53
Personhood Act (2010, 2012), Oklahoma,
84, 85, 92
Peru, 156n56
petition for an abortion in El Salvador:
anencephaly diagnosis, 17; argument against a medical need for an
abortion, 32–34; background, 13–14;
Beatriz's decision to not get sterilized,
38–39; Beatriz's living conditions,
36–38; Beatriz's relationship with her
husband, 39–40; belief that Beatriz became pregnant irresponsibly,
35–36; constitutional right to life
consideration, 17, 19, 27, 28, 30–31;
doctrine of double-effect and, 32,
149n29; experts assembled by the
IML, 22–24; filing of the petition to
the court, 19–20; ideological basis
of each sides' arguments, 41; IML's
criteria for permitting an abortion,
21; IML's examination and conclusion, 25–26; IML's status and
staffing, 21–22; ironies in Beatriz's
medical status, 28–29; lack of legal
support for an interruption, 17; law
of self-defense and, 34–35; law's "immediate danger" to life requirement,
29–34; legal jeopardy for the attending doctors, 35; legal rationale for
maintaining non-viable pregnancies,
19; media harassment of Beatriz and
her family, 20–21; medical committee's recommendation, 17; medical
impact of pregnancy for Beatriz, 16;
medical jeopardy caused by the court's
decision, 28–29; obstetric profession's
position, 23–24, 148n16; point of law
that allowed the doctors to intervene,
35, 149nn32–33; political firestorm

over the case, 26–27; public response to her petition, 20; required treatment for high-risk pregnancies, 17–19; stress and vulnerabilities in Beatriz's life, 39, 40; technicality that limited the defense's case, 27; timeline of the courts' decisions, 19, 20, 25, 26, 27–28

Pinochet, Augusto, 7

Planned Parenthood, 1, 2, 4, 114, 159*n*11

Planned Parenthood v. Casey, 4, 114, 159*n*11

poor women: cost factor in abortion, 9, 79, 87, 125; cost factor of motherhood, 97–98, 106, 107, 109–11; governmental priorities regarding the costs of caring for children, 109; impact of abortion laws on, 66, 75, 78–79, 113, 115–16, 117, 123, 156*n*57; impact of restricting federal funding for abortion, 113; indirect consequences of a ban on abortion, 136–37; options for medical care, 51; pregnancy's impact on existing vulnerabilities for, 1–2, 3–4, 108–9; public policy's impact on poor women's mothering choices, 111

preeclampsia, 16

pregnant addicts: circumstances leading to drug use, 3; inadequacy of drug treatment centers for, 4; lack of access to abortion, 4; relevancy of abortion's legal status for, 4–5, 6–7; responses to pregnancy, 3–4; societal fear of drug-addicted babies, 3

Privileges and Immunities Clause, US Constitution, 123

pro-choice: definition of, 12; framing of the potential outcomes of criminalizing abortion, 119, 127; majority of states' position on, 122; political power of constituent groups, 75; position on abortion, 141; reaction to a post-abortion conviction, 132–33, 164*n*36; reaction to prosecutions, 130

pro-life movement: alliance with faith-based communities, 72; campaign for a constitutional amendment, 160*n*11; lack of a consensus on what is acceptable, 122; lawmakers' testing of their power to regulate abortion, 113, 158–59*n*11; positions on punishment for women, 126–27, 142*n*16; power to influence like-minded people, 87; pro-life versus antiabortion, 103; reaction to a post-abortion conviction, 132–33, 164*n*36; reaction to Oklahoma's Personhood Act failure, 84, 85, 92; services focus of a crisis pregnancy center, 103

public choice theory, 92–93

Ramirez, Jorge, 32

rape: abortion exception for, 10, 36, 61, 78, 86, 87, 89, 113, 122; absence of an abortion exception for, 17, 43; legislators' positions on exemptions for, 87; vulnerability of women and, 64, 104

Reagan, Leslie, 127

Reynolds, Mike, 80, 85, 139

Right to Life, 102

Roberts, Ellen, 102. *See also* Birth Choice

Roberts, Sarah, 115

Rodriguez, Delmer, 30

Rodriguez, Maria Isabel, 26

Roe v. Wade, 4, 71; allowance for legal abortions if overturned, 120, 122; concept of fetal viability in the right to abort, 121; constitutional basis of, 120–21; focus of abortion-related prosecutions, pre-*Roe*, 127, 162*n*20; impact of *Roe* on choices made, 112; predictions of the political impact of a reversal of, 88–89, 93; pre-*Roe* mortalities from abortion, 124; pro-life states' responses to "undue burden test," 114; timeline of post-*Roe* rulings, 158–59*n*11

Rose Day rallies, 73–74

Rose Home, 103–5

Rosen, Mark D., 161*n*8
RU-486, 45

"second victim" exception to abortion
    prosecutions, 129–30, 131, 133–34
self-abortion, 45, 64, 119, 126, 128,
    162–63*nn*22–23, 163*n*32
Sí a la Vida, 26
South Carolina, 134
South Dakota, 158*n*8, 163*n*23
Southern Baptist Convention (SBC): in-
    volvement in abortion politics, 72–74;
    political lobbying, 74; position on
    abortion in 1973, 70
Spiropoulos, Andrew, 70, 77
states and abortion: constitutionality of
    states' anti-abortion laws, 114, 120,
    122, 158–59*n*11; pro-life states' re-
    sponses to "undue burden test," 114;
    state-mandated misinformation about
    abortion, 145–46*n*5; states' enacting
    of abortion-related laws, 6, 145*n*5;
    states' enforcement of abortion laws,
    126, 161*n*13. *See also* Oklahoma;
    United States
Steele, Kris, 93, 141; legislative record,
    91; post-politician ministry, 89–90;
    tabling of the Personhood Bill, 89, 92
Sunstein, Cass, 42, 43, 138
Supreme Court, El Salvador, 21, 27–28,
    35
Supreme Court, US: concept of fetal
    viability in the right to abort, 121;
    legal battles over abortion, 4; *Planned
    Parenthood v. Casey*, 4, 114, 159*n*11;
    pro-life states' responses to "undue
    burden test," 114; *Roe* decision (see
    Roe v. Wade); *Webster v. Reproduc-
    tive Health Services*, 159*n*11

TEEM (The Education and Employment
    Ministry), 89
teen pregnancies, 64, 136–37,
    165*nn*43-44
Texas, 145–46*n*5
trisomy 18, 79

Trump, Donald, 126, 162*n*16
Tulsans for Life, 71

undue burden test, 4, 114
United States: abortion tourism in, 123;
    black market in illegal abortions,
    125–26; case of a women charged
    with feticide and child neglect,
    132–33, 164*n*33, 164*n*36; cases in
    which the law sees the woman as a
    criminal, 130–31; claim that banning
    abortion reduces abortion rates, 137;
    concept of fetal viability in the right
    to abort, 121; constitutionality of
    abortion (*see Roe v. Wade*); cost factor
    in illegal abortion, 125; definition
    of an illegal abortion, 131, 163*n*32;
    demographics of women prosecuted
    for pregnancy-related crimes, 135,
    165*n*42; evidence of increased homo-
    geneity of American communities, 90;
    focus of abortion-related prosecutions,
    pre-*Roe*, 127, 162*n*20; framing of the
    potential outcomes of criminalizing
    abortion, 119; frequency of prosecu-
    tions of women for illegal abortions,
    128–29, 131; hospital reports of dan-
    gerous self-abortion attempts, 126; im-
    pact of abortion laws on poor women
    (*see* poor women); indirect conse-
    quences of a ban, 136–37; lack of a
    pro-life consensus on what is accept-
    able, 122; laws against self-abortion,
    128, 131, 162–63*nn*22-23, 163*n*32;
    laws regarding patient confidentiality,
    47, 152*n*17, 152*n*20; moral basis for
    opposition to abortion, 3, 41, 81,
    83–84, 85; moral justification derived
    from anti-abortion laws, 137; Okla-
    homa's abortion laws (*see* Oklahoma);
    pattern of law enforcement of abor-
    tion regulations, 134; political power
    of constituent groups, 75; pre-*Roe*
    mortalities from abortion, 124; pro-
    lifers' positions on punishment for
    women, 126–27, 142*n*16; reactions to

a post-abortion conviction, 132–33, 164*n*36; "second victim" exception to abortion prosecutions, 129–30, 131, 133–34; socioeconomic status' role in the risks of illegal abortion, 124–25; state-mandated misinformation about abortion, 145–46*n*5; states' enacting of abortion-related laws, 6, 145*n*5; states' enforcement of anti-abortion laws, 126, 161*n*13; states' power to allow or ban abortion, 120, 122; targeting of the poor in public hospitals, 66, 156*n*57; teen pregnancy and, 136–37; unconstitutionality of a complete ban on abortion, 121
US Supreme Court. *See* Supreme Court, US
Utah, 115

in vitro fertilization, 91

Wallace, David Foster, 2
Webster v. Reproductive Health Services, 159*n*11
Wilke, John C., 106
women who killed their children: attitudes toward abortion, 5, 101; Eva's story, 5–6; sentiments toward motherhood, 5, 6; wrongful convictions after miscarriages, 56, 58, 61, 62, 131, 133; wrongful convictions investigations, 60–62
World Health Organization (WHO), 45, 150*n*2, 152*n*12

zygote, 41, 150*n*37